International Textbooks in Education

We Do Not Throw Rocks at the Teacher!

We Do No

at the

Illustrations by Eric Peavy

Throw Rocks Teacher!

Devoted to the teacher goal of establishing
classroom control and/or discipline

KATHERINE C. LA MANCUSA

International Textbook Company, Scranton, Pennsylvania

Third Printing, February 1969

Copyright ©, 1966, by International Textbook Company. All rights reserved. Printed in the United States of America by The Haddon Craftsmen, Inc., at Scranton, Pennsylvania.
Library of Congress Catalog Card Number: 66-16243.

Standard Book Number 7002 2059 3

To
Donna Angela

Introduction

For those teachers for whom this book is written and for those teachers for whom this book will have an appeal, no introduction is necessary.

The establishment of sound practices in the development of classroom control and/or discipline is a never-ending process which begins rightfully on the first minute of the first day in the new school semester. As one successful teacher said, "I never took my hat off until now, and I have been here for twenty years!"

Creative classroom control comes from first understanding and accepting the worth of the individual. A further commitment is needed toward the development of a child's self-concept, in providing the kinds of experiences which would allow him to both test and limit his social actions. When he learns his positive social potential in the development of his social self, he frees both himself and his teacher, so that together they may spread their wings and fly!

KATHERINE C. LA MANCUSA

Acknowledgments

Gratitude is expressed to the following for their invaluable help in the preparation of this manuscript:

To Mr. Eric Peavy, who rendered the line drawings for this work. His all-round giftedness, his self-direction with a given title, his interpretation of humor, his craftsmanship as an artist, together with his dependability in meeting a deadline have enhanced this book more than words can adequately express.

To Dr. Arthur F. Corey, State Executive Secretary of the California Teachers Association, who has always been a source of inspiration to countless educators. For this, and his generosity in granting his permission to use a story contained in Chapter 12, I offer my humble and heartfelt, "Thank you."

To International Textbook Company, particularly to Mr. Kenneth Gromlich, Mr. Kay Chamberlain, and to Mr. Gerald Stashak for their continued interest and support of my writings —in this, my second publication.

To an indulgent family, and my best audience, who have continually demonstrated their selflessness in providing the environment for productive writing.

To the hundreds—possibly thousands—of students who have been in my classrooms both in schools and in colleges. Their constancy in holding up reflective mirrors taught their teacher far more than she could ever have hoped to have taught them.

Finally, and devoutly, to a merciful Lord and God who has continued to demonstrate to this author that "His eye" *is* indeed "on the sparrow."

KATHERINE C. LA MANCUSA

Special Note

In all instances, unless otherwise noted, all quotations, names of teachers and children, as well as narration illustrating specific experiences, are drawn from the author's imagination and bear no resemblance either to persons living or dead or to experiences in the past, in the present, or in the future.

Contents

When Common Sense Appears Uncommon . . . 1

How Many Bells for a Fire Drill, Again? . . . 11

On Being Pro, Not Anti 19

Has Anyone Seen My Keys? 25

Contentment Is a Pretty Room 31

Who Will Clean Our Lovely Snake Cage? . . 39

The Broken-Crayon Monitor 45

Now Enter Billy Bully 51

We Do Not Throw Rocks at the Teacher! . . . 59

On Giving In for the Moment 65

A Pox on Him Who Finishes Too Fast! . . . 71

The Letter That Goes Home (Again)! 77

The Perennial Offender 83

Efficacious Bouncing 89

The Golden Rule Remains Golden 95

The Teacher Is Not a Peer Group 101

But I Really Want to Be Loved! 107

Trippingly on the Tongue 113

Veni, Vidi, Vici! 121

On Hoisting the White Flag 125

It's Clean-Up Time! 131

That Smashingly Quiet Hour 137

When Nothing Works 141

A Parent-ing We Will Go! 149

It's Tuesday Already! 157

Teacher Conservation Program 165

These Teachers I Try to Forget 173

These Teachers I Will Always Remember . . 181

But You Don't Look Like a Teacher! 187

Nota Bene! 197

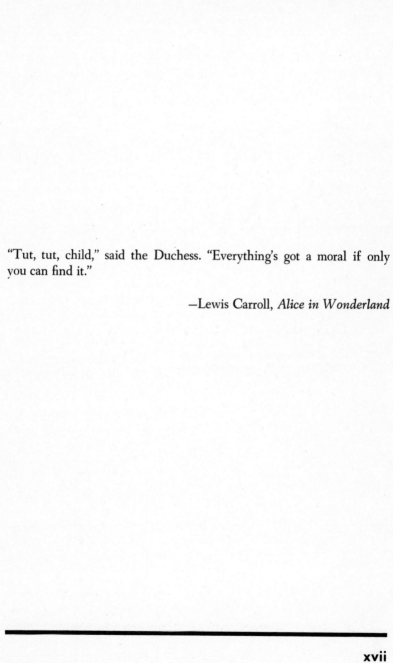

"Tut, tut, child," said the Duchess. "Everything's got a moral if only you can find it."

—Lewis Carroll, *Alice in Wonderland*

1 When Common Sense Appears Uncommon

In the enlightened vernacular of the contemporary educator, the word *discipline* has been supplanted by the word *control*. Few teachers would be prone to argue in depth over this point of semantics, for either term is understood, and either term is universally respected.

Practical educators know that evaluation and assessment in this area can never be quasi or intermediary. When a teacher *has* classroom control, he *knows* it. When a teacher does not have classroom control, he knows it with the same degree of certainty.

Some neophytes in the profession, and the so-called ineffectual teachers, are characterized by their halting, malfunctioning, and oftentimes retrogressive attempts to establish a firm footing in the classroom. What worked smashingly well yesterday, no longer worked today!

They can be likened to the beginning driver who alternately overdrives and underdrives his car. They assume a smooth motion and then a jerking motion; never being quite sure, in their own minds, why each stage developed. How can one grasp the wheel lightly and, at the same time, maintain complete control?

Insensitivities exist and flourish among the inexperienced and ineffectual teachers, for they are no more sure of what their responses should be than they are sure of where their threshold for tolerance should lie. In having learned how to swallow camels they have forgotten how *not* to choke on gnats.

They may ask themselves, "Shall I be firm today, or shall I be benign? Shall I show them that I am displeased with them, or shall I pretend that I do not care?"

Such teachers cannot be considered eclectic but, rather, *neutralized* by a deadly homogenization of ambiguities. Rendered immobile with no sure feelings for direction nor felt reasons for alternatives, they become *greyed* with indecisiveness.

How does it happen? Are these teachers blameless or are they to blame? Did they not garner exemplary grades in method's courses? Did they not experience peer teaching?

Simple answers to complex questions can seldom be offered, no more than a college lectern can hope to give to the teaching candidate all of the realities of his role. The promulgation of the teaching task, in its day-by-day execution, must be independently experienced in order to be fully understood. College preparation helps, but so does learning by doing and extracting the wheat from the chaff.

Some teachers may be hampered rather than helped by their psychology courses. Their *smatterings of psychology*, by any mean evaluative process, often appears to be more academic than understood. While it is wholly commendable to deal with the psychology of the problem, it is wholly uncommendable for a teacher to attempt to be a diagnostician and offer therapy on a pseudopsychiatric level.

The very real task of helping children to understand their social limitations relative to classroom behavior is often set aside in lieu of *psychological tinkering*. Through misguided feelings of pity and compassion, initial errors in judgment are made by stepping between the act and the consequences for the act. Hence, all reasonable guidlines for norms are neatly rationalized away.

Let it be said at the outset that the classroom was never intended to serve as a therapy center wherein the suspected "disturbed child" may be permitted to bang on boxes in order to rid himself of his hostilities. Under these circumstances, it would be altogether fair to assume that a fine growth of hostilities may develop in the adjusted child *and in the teacher as well!*

The classroom belongs to *all* children, including the majority, who are well adjusted and who adhere to established standards for behavior. Indeed, the classroom even belongs to the teacher. And, why not? He has to live there and function in his role!

Unfortunately, in most discussions and writings relating to classroom control, the teacher's needs and tolerances have been forgotten and have been swept under the rug. In most instances, unfortunately, those who do the *sweeping,* are the armchair philosophers and *not* the practical practitioners of the trade.

While it cannot be denied that a teacher is both selfless and altruistic, in sheer terms of practicality, good mental health, and longevity, it must be remembered that the teacher is a person too; his is *not* an expendable role.

There is no common mold for operational facility in teaching. Total adherence to the philosophy of personalism, which would respect individual differences among children, would at the same time respect individual differences among teachers as well. In this frame of reference, one teacher might work most effectively, for example, in a laissez-faire classroom climate, while another might work most effectively in a more structured one. There is nothing wrong with this statement of fact. That it has been aired publicly, may cause some to gasp audibly. Yet, in countless administrator's files, documented records attest to the fact that each kind of teacher can make his contribution and each can be considered a valued member of a teaching staff.

The teacher who attempts to perform in his role, under philosophies which have been either unwisely imposed or naïvely selected, will falter at his operational task.

"To thine ownself, be true!" is a valid guideline for application, provided, of course, that the door is left ajar for the possibility of change through maturation in the continual process of self-evaluation.

It would be foolish to assert that a given teacher would never change or modify his approach to control as his experiences are gained and assimilated. Reins that have been held rather tightly initially may be loosened later, either in terms of a given semester or of a given number of teaching years. The reverse, among the inexperienced and ineffectual teachers, has seldom if ever held true.

The classroom has been defined as an environment for learning. It has been said, time and time again, that learning cannot take place in chaos. Therefore, there must exist among experienced and effectual teachers certain common principles for practical application which would assure and maintain a reasonable climate for that learning and subsequent growth.

Assuming that such direction does exist and that teachers have applied these common principles, what can the teacher do with, or for, that child who is the chronic offender, on whose total personality, the application of established principles has the effect of a gnat striking an elephant?

First of all, a teacher must deal with behavioral problems in terms he can understand. His training, knowledgeableness, experience, maturity, and his instincts all work together in the projection of expectations for healthy and realistic social behavior. When the sum total of the teacher's efforts appear to be ineffectual for a particular child and when this child continues to demonstrate negative and devious social behavior in consistently falling short of the expected norm, then the *time* and the *reason* for seeking professional help would appear propitious.

The *whys* and *wherefores* of a child's chronic misbehavior, in terms of depth perception, are best left in the capable hands of the counselors, psychologists, and psychiatrists. While a teacher has been called a lay practitioner in the area of counseling, he is not a specialist in the area of human behavior. Conversely, none of these specialists is *that* teacher. Each must work together to develop understanding and respect for the other's role if the child's behavioral pattern is to change and emerge with fruition.

In seeking the help of a specialist in the school setting, a word of caution is appropriate in terms of one's adherence to policy and procedure. More than one well-meaning teacher has embarrassed both himself and his school district by saying, "Madame, your child needs a psychiatrist!"

A teacher cannot say this, no more than he can diagnose orthopedic handicaps in making recommendations for bone surgery. However apparent the need, the road for the teacher is much *more deliberate,* infinitely *more exploratory,* and assuredly *less diagnostic.*

No one area of professional endeavor presents more reason for soul searching, toward total commitment, than that of teaching. When approximately one-half of the nation's population is included in the age range of 25 years and younger, it will never be enough to say, "I know how I am here." Rather, it needs be, "I know *why*."

Albeit that classroom control in the total educational process is a means toward an end and not the end in itself, it cannot be denied that the area of behavioral discipline is fraught with fear and helpless resignation toward abject failure.

It would appear that everyone has a voice in placing the blame on somebody or something in this rather generalized social malaise. Comments range from, "Kids aren't what they used to be," to, "We're headed toward anarchy."

Parents blame the teachers, the times, and/or, other parents.

Teachers blame the parents, the times, and/or, other teachers.

An industrialist was quoted recently as having said, "Juvenile deliquents begin in kindergarten!"

Newspapers have carried banner headlines proclaiming, "KIDS GIVE TEACHERS A WORSE TIME!"

Individuals, times, schools, and systems appear guilt laden. When the last name has been called and the last of the blame has been laid, cold retrospect brings forth emotionless evaluation. Not *all* individuals are at fault. The times are not fruitless for *all* people. The schools are not *all* bad and neither are the systems which contain them *all* bad.

What then, is it?

Does the truth lie in the *cracks* of what *appear to be* blatantly true areas for concern? And/or is it an individual matter which is individually centered, individually interpreted, and individually promulgated?

A teacher might say, "If all parents were successful in creating a readiness for behavioral discipline and respect for authority, the teacher's role would, ideally, be one of reinforcement."

The parent might reverse this statement and counter, "If all teachers were successful in reinforcing that which has been begun in the home, then parents ideally could create a readiness for behavioral discipline and respect for authority."

The question might be asked, "What *is* successful readiness for discipline and what *is* successful respect for authority?" Shall we ask two parents? Do we get two different interpretations?

What, then, *is* successful reinforcement? Must a teacher split himself 30 different ways in order to promulgate 30 different home interpretations? Or must a teacher, in all sane reality, say in the end, "It is *my* interpretation, based upon *my* training, *my* knowledge, *my* experience, *my* maturity, and *my* instincts which will work together in projecting expectations for healthy and realistic social behavior."

The challenge for teachers lies in beginning at the beginning, in accepting the worth of individual differences in a democratic society and then striving to find the means for a social working realization, not only in ones, but in groups, and in wholes. With diversification of personality remaining apparent (even in grouping), the teacher begins to weld and to bond into a unified whole. Eventually the whole is acting as one, collectively stated and collectively addressed. One can liken the process to the creation of a collage in the art area, wherein varied papers of different shapes are glued down onto a common ground. While diversification of materials is apparent and is never lost in the surface treatment, these individual papers and shapes have, nevertheless, *taken on another character*, relating now *to other papers* in areas of dominance and subordination and, finally, to the *one and unified whole* of the design in its final configuration and cohesiveness.

The neophyte and the ineffectual teacher might well ask, "What hope, then, is there for me?"

The experienced and effectual teacher might answer, "Hope lies in understanding and accepting that all is *not* hopeless. Sound practices in the establishment of classroom control are sometimes mere tricks of the trade and, at other times, just plain common sense with a firm commitment to the *reasonableness* of student behavior."

For those teachers who have never learned the tricks, and for those teachers who believe like Horace Greeley, that "common sense is very uncommon," these following chapters are written and presented as a guide.

2 How Many Bells for a Fire Drill, Again?

Knowledgeableness will make its own unique contribution to control and will aid immeasurably in one's quest for high gear operational facility in the classroom.

With first things first, the inexperienced teacher (as well as the experienced teacher in a new school setting) should orient himself thoroughly in all matters pertaining to policy and procedure. This would encompass the district and school policy and procedure as well as state education codes or state school laws.

Lack of familiarity in these areas acts as a deterrent in the establishment of classroom control, for any interruption in the school day, no matter how small and seemingly insignificant, demands the immediate dispatch and direction of the teacher, with an economy of recall. When answers to questions are known, a teacher's direction is swift and the important area of *transition* is unfalteringly smooth.

One's ability to adjust to the realities of his school society, in becoming a functioning member of a teaching staff, would bring about a positive demonstration of both resourcefulness and self reliance. This would negate the somewhat natural proclivity toward finding total dependence upon one's colleagues and administrators. Often it is possible to attend orientation meetings within the school district, and at other times it is possible to obtain needed information from teacher's handbooks.

However one builds his knowledgeableness, it should be done early enough to forestall chaos when a crisis occurs and thoroughly enough to forestall those long periods of indecisiveness when immediate direction is needed.

Familiarity in the area of policy and procedure is a decided measuring stick for a teacher's total effectiveness in his role.

Typically, a new teacher in a new school setting would ask himself and seek the answers to the following questions:

1. What are the names of the administrative officers in the school district, and what are their specific roles?

2. Who are the Board members? What powers are invested in them, and when do they meet?

3. What is the projected district school calendar in terms of holidays, vacations, and numbers of teaching days?

4. What district statements exist relative to teaching philosophy and matters of control?

5. What are the district policies relative to teacher evaluation, rehiring, tenure, salary increases, in-service courses, sick leave, and retirement?

6. Is there a group health plan which is available to teachers within the school district? Other types of insurance?

7. What are the physical boundaries for the school district?

8. How many schools are contained within the school district, and what kinds?

9. What district facilities exist in terms of special schools or classrooms for the exceptional child, including: gifted, mentally retarded, accoustically handicapped, visually handicapped, orthopedically handicapped, neurologically handicapped, aphasic, cerebral palsied, and emotionally disturbed?

10. Who are the district specialists in the educational program for the exceptional child?

11. If no programs for the exceptional child exist, what special teaching materials and aids are available for the classroom teacher?

12. What other specialists are employed by the school district, such as: counselors, psychologists, psychiatrists, medical doctors, ophthalmologists, *and* consultants in the special areas such as art, music, science, physical education, and general curriculum? What is their schedule for school visitations, and how does one avail himself of their services? Through what channels must one go? The school principal? Others?

13. What are the district facilities for audiovisual aids and equipment and for professional libraries?

14. What does the state education code specifically say relative to mandatory subject areas which must be contained within a district's curriculum pattern?

15. What curriculum patterns exist in the school district relative to courses of study? Is scope and sequence, in terms of grade levels, specifically delineated?

16. Is the teacher committed to stay within the confines of the district course of study pattern? What latitudes may he take? For example, may one correlate subject areas such as science and health? Social studies and reading?

17. What is the prescribed minimum period of time which must be devoted to each subject area per day and per week?

18. Does a district or school policy exist which relates to the specificity of symbols which are to be used for grading purposes? Are these uniform throughout the grades?

19. Are teachers expected to send home a minimum number of graded papers each week? In all areas?

20. When and how often are reporting periods conducted? Are report cards used? Parent conferences? Both?

21. What policies exist relative to promotions? Are they based on academic achievement? Social factors? Both?

22. When are students promoted? Biannually? Annually?

23. What policies exist relative to retaining a child in the same grade and/or accelerating a child to a higher grade? What criterion is used? What kinds of evidence must be collected for both?

24. Is there a districtwide or schoolwide testing program? Which tests are used and for what purpose? When are they given, by whom, and how often? Who scores them? Teacher? Psychometrist? Machine scored?

25. Is there an existing policy toward homework? How much is to be given? How little? None?

26. Which school rules exist relative to student behavior on the playground, in the halls, and in the cafeteria?

27. When a teacher is on duty, what does he do when infractions exist relative to established policies for behavior in the halls, playground, and in the cafeteria?

28. How is the yard-duty schedule distributed? Posted? Put on post boxes?

29. Are students expected to form lines at all times when entering or leaving the classroom? More informal?

30. What does a teacher do when a child is seriously injured on the playground? Administer first aid? Send a student to the office for help?

31. What latitudes and restrictions exist relative to a teacher administering first aid?

32. Who are the children who are exempt from physical examinations and/or health programs because of personal family convictions? To what degree are these convictions honored?

33. What does a teacher do for or with that child who

comes to school with a fever or general malaise?

34. What does a teacher do when a child becomes ill in his classroom?

35. Is there a school health program for physical examinations, eye examinations, ear examinations, inoculations, polio shots, skin-patch tests, and fluoroscopic examinations? Must every student participate in these programs?

36. How does a teacher report absences? Daily? Weekly? Monthly?

37. What does a teacher do when a child has been absent from school for several days? Call his home? Report it to the office? Report it to the school nurse?

38. What policy exists for those children who are often tardy and often absent (both for reasons of illness and for reasons other than illness)?

39. What policy exists toward parental requests to take their children out of school for reasons other than illness?

40. Are parents expected to write excuses when students are tardy or absent?

41. Are parents required to report to the office before visiting the classrooms?

42. How does the bell system operate? What are the signals, and at what time do the bells ring for the beginning of school, recesses, lunch periods, and closing? Are there warning bells?

43. What are the signals for fire drills, earthquakes, and air raids? How does a teacher proceed? Where does he take his students, and/or what does he instruct his students to do?

44. Are there minimum teaching days at times of rain or snow? Where do the children play and eat at recess and lunch periods on these days?

45. At what time is the teacher expected to be in his class-

room in the morning? What is the earliest time for leaving in the evening? The latest hour?

46. Where do the students cross the street in the morning, at noon, and at night? Is there a school traffic patrol? A police officer? Are children allowed to cross the streets unsupervised?

47. What special supervision problems are imposed upon that teacher who detains students after school hours? Must he call the child's parent and tell him that his child is detained? Must he accompany that child across the street?

48. Is there a bus available for students who live in distant areas? What is its schedule for arriving and leaving?

49. Is there a school hot-lunch program in the cafeteria? Where do the children with bag lunches eat?

50. Is there a milk-and-cracker program for the children in the primary grades? What does it cost? Who collects the money? When and where are the milk and crackers distributed?

51. Is there a policy which would discourage the celebration of birthdays within the classroom?

52. Is there a limit to the number of classroom parties within a given semester's period?

53. Is there a banking program within the school? How is it conducted and on what day?

54. Is there a district provision for making accident insurance policies available to parents at a minimal cost?

55. How may a teacher make contact with his student's former teacher in order to discuss the characteristics of the class he will be receiving and to be made aware of existing grouping within specific subject areas?

56. Where are the cumulative records for individual students kept? What information must a teacher add to these records and at what time?

57. Where is the textbook room within the school? Which textbooks have been adopted within the district? Which are the supplementary texts?

58. Is there a school library? What policies exist for its use?

59. Where is the supply closet within the school? How does a teacher obtain his supplies? Through requisition forms? Through an open-door system?

60. Is there a policy relative to the necessity for teachers to write daily lesson plans? Weekly plans? Projected monthly plans? Are these reviewed? By whom?

61. How, and at what time, does a teacher report his own illness and inability to teach on a given day?

62. Are there buses available for field trips? How many field trips are allocated to each teacher per semester? Is parental permission necessary for field trips? What permission forms exist? Where are these forms located? Must a first-aid kit be taken on every field trip?

63. Who are the members of the school teaching faculty, custodial staff, secretarial staff, and special services personnel?

64. Is there a PTA or Parent-Faculty organization? When and how often do they meet?

65. Is there a professional teachers' organization within the school district? Who are their officers? When and how often do they meet?

3 On Being Pro, Not Anti

Policy has been defined as "practical wisdom"; procedure as a "definite course of action." Together they may be considered as regulatory measures which are preventive and supportive, not obstructing and impeding.

Through the individual efforts of a teaching staff, in terms of adherence to policy and procedural matters, total school operational facility is collectively stated and collectively evaluated. In this frame of reference, a school principal once said, "Give me a teacher who is supportive and one who will not challenge matters of policy and procedure—at least not in his first three weeks of employment!"

This administrator was saying, in effect, that when policy exists, there is usually a good reason for that policy; when procedure exists, there is usually a good reason for that procedure. Seldom are they formulated under administrative whim or fancy. Historical precedent, in terms of experience and need in the problem-solving area, lies as the bedrock foundational element in all school matters which articulate practical wisdom and definite courses of action.

By way of illustration, let us suppose that a newly hired teacher made an appointment with his administrator in order to state his objections to the established policy of teaching reading through the consistent adoption of the same reading series of textbooks. "My personal philosophy," he said, "lies in the area of teaching reading through an interest-centered individualized reading approach. I do not believe that the consistent adoption of the same reading series is an effective method for teaching reading."

The principal listened to the teacher and then said, "I have an appreciation for your philosophy, and I have an appreciation for the worth of the individualized reading approach, under certain circumstances, but in this school district we adhere to the policy of teaching reading through our adopted series and correlated teacher manuals. We do this for purposes of continuity in our large school district, both for the continuity of skill development and vocabulary reinforcement and for the sequential progression toward reading proficiency in comprehension. While I believe that a skilled teacher can do the same thing in the interest-centered individualized reading approach, I cannot condone its practice inasmuch as it would run counter to district policy. I do not dictate school policy, I expedite it. Do you understand my position?" he asked the teacher.

No, the teacher did not understand, but leaned forward in his chair to once again state his objections to the established policy of teaching reading through the adoption of a reading series.

"You do not understand what I am saying," said the administrator. "I do not necessarily disagree with your premise, but I disagree with your conclusion. My personal feelings are totally divorced from district policy in this matter. If you would have me disavow district policy and procedure, I would cease to serve as an effective administrator. It would be fair to assume, under these circumstances, that I might be encouraged to look for alternate pastures in which to graze, just as a teacher ·who ceases to function under existing policies might be similarly encouraged."

Basic in a teacher's desire to establish classroom control, is a commitment toward support and follow-through in the regu-

latory aspects of the school society. It begins with a respect for authority in maintaining cooperative working relationships in the total school setting, and it ends with fruition when rules and regulations and or policies and procedures are understood in terms of being facilitating agents toward the betterment of all, and toward the detriment of none.

Matters of policy and procedure can be defined as a type of school law which is mandatory, not permissive, in character. Such laws within the school setting are wholly compatible with one's concept of a democratic society wherein social law is accepted as a functional reality. Lawbreakers in a social order governed by rules and regulations *detract* from the total freedom of *everyone,* not only of themselves, just as teachers who are careless or indifferent to the existing laws governing their school society are a detriment to everyone, not only to themselves. Students, parents, teachers, administrators, secretaries, custodians, bus drivers, and special services personnel feel the backlash of *double standards* when rules are made to be broken.

Respect for authority is gleaned by students through incidental learnings. It is not, "Do as I say; not as I do." Rather, it is, "Do as I am!"

When students become aware of teachers displaying a lack of respect for either the administration or for established policy and procedural matters, they may well choose to relate their observations to their own classroom behavior. "If the teacher can be disobedient, why can't we?" they may ask. Students *can* be disobedient and *will* be disobedient under the existing circumstances, for imitation is one of the strongest theories in learning, particularly when it is reinforced by an authoritative figure. Students are good imitators.

It is tragic, of course, that these teacher-student attitudes create a readiness for anarchy where no rules for social order are either evidenced or respected. Supervision in the hallways, cafeteria, and on the playground becomes more difficult; eventually it spreads to the classrooms. Children begin to query their teachers by saying, *"His* teacher lets him do it! Why can't *I?"*

It is entirely possible within a given school wing, where six teachers operate, to have but one arbitrary teacher contribute to chaos for all concerned. Sometimes, in a school society, the self-styled liberators of the oppressed and/or the arbitrary teachers find their apex of development shortly after their tenure is granted. After permanency is assured, the most docile and supportive of teachers have been known to suddenly develop a yearning to wear the administrator's hat and to begin to make administrative decisions relative to modification of policy and procedural matters. This confusion of roles is possibly one of the most frustrating of administrative problems, for seldom are such teachers confronted with the reality of accepting the legal responsibility for their actions, when things go wrong and a principal must justify the existence of his *weakest link.*

"I do not teach in the classrooms," an administrator said, "but I expedite matters so that teaching can be done; conversely, teachers do not make administrative decisions, but expedite them so that administrative functions can reach fruition in making the teaching load lighter, not more cumbersome. It represents a round robin of cooperative endeavor." He continued, "When I fail in my role, teaching becomes more difficult; when teachers fail in their roles, administration becomes more difficult. It is true," he said reflectively, "that a school's total effectiveness is as strong as its weakest link."

Regulatory laws govern all societies, from the most primitive to the most sophisticated, and the freedom that exists in a democratic society finds fruition not in a dearth, but in a plethora of accepted responsibilities.

Governor Pat Brown of California said on December 10, 1964, "In a society governed by law, a decision to defy the law must include a decision to accept the consequences."

In a school society, it is *basic* to accept one's reponsibilities in matters of policy and procedure. This does not imply that governing operational laws within that school society cannot be changed or modified, simplified or extended when the need arises and when the existing statements have become cumbersome and outdated. The committee-study approach is but one of many satisfactory methods in seeking solutions which would update and make school policies more effective and realistic. The attitude in the committee-study approach between teachers and administrators is positive, not negative; rational and not irrational; supportive and not insubordinate. It seeks solutions to common problems and makes a mature and dignified contribution toward education for all.

4 Has Anyone Seen My Keys?

Miss Daftly is demonstrating a papier-mâché technique to her second grade class. She begins to crush the newspaper in order to create her basic armature form. "See how I am doing this, children?" she asks. "Do you see how I made the two little ears for my bunny rabbit?"

The children nodded.

"Boy, Miss Daftly," says one little tot, "that's really *neat!*"

"Of course," says another, "our teacher is an *artist!*"

Miss Daftly smiles with satisfaction. There is no doubt in her mind but that *this* is her lucky day, for, you see, it is sometimes difficult for her to make bunny ears that look like bunny ears. Sometimes her bunny ears look like elephant ears. "You see what I am doing, children? I am going to tie these bunny ears to the head of my bunny rabbit. Wait until I get my string. Where is my string? Children, did any of you see my string?"

"Noooooo, Misssss Daftlyyyyyy," the children chorus.

"But, that is impossible! I always have string when I make my bunny rabbits. I—."

Yes, it *is* possible. In cold retrospect, Miss Daftly remembers. She forgot to put the string on the table with the rest of the materials. Now she will have to unlock the cabinet in order to get some. Where are her keys? "Children, has anyone seen my keys?"

"Nooooooo, Misssss Daftlyyyyyy," the second graders chorus again.

"Oh dear," she sighs. "Tommy, will you go to Miss Green's

room and ask her if I may borrow some of her string?"

Tommy arises and steadfastly makes his way to the door. He opens it, walks out, and closes the door softly behind him.

But lo! A moment later, the door opens again, and there stands Tommy. "What room is she in?" he asks.

Miss Daftly appears somewhat exasperated, and there is a slight edge to her voice as she responds, "Miss Green is in Room 2!—No, wait Tommy, I believe she is in Room 3—no—! Children, do you know Miss Green's room number?"

"She is in Room 5," says one little moppet.

"No," says another, shaking his head from side to side, "she is in room eleven-teen."

"No, silly, that's *our* room!"

"Oh dear," Miss Daftly says, "I will have to look it up!" She puts down the bunny rabbit and the two bunny ears and pulls the school directory from her desk drawer. "Miss Green is in Room 4," she says wearily.

Again Tommy opens the door, walks out, and closes the door softly behind him.

Miss Daftly picks up her crumpled newspaper rabbit and the two crumpled newspaper rabbit ears, and attempts to place them in approximately the same position that she had them in before. But alas, the crumpled newspaper rabbit has begun to uncrumple and the crumpled newspaper rabbit ears have begun to assume forms which are quite un-rabbit-ear-looking.

"You're ruining it, Miss Daftly," warns a child.

"My dear Anastasia," says Miss Daftly authoritatively, "your teacher *knows* what she is doing. Be patient now, and I will make the bunny rabbit look nice again."

"Miss Daftly!" a child's voice calls out "Billy hit me!"

"Billy, did *you* hit Marcia?"

"No, I did not. Marcia is a liar."

"I am not a liar! You did *too* hit me!" So saying, Marcia lets fly a smart crack to the boy's cranium area.

The teacher's muffled voice comes from under sheaves of crumpled newspapers, "Stop it! Stop it, I say! If you children are not going to pay attention, I will have to stop making this bunny rabbit!"

"Who cares?" says the classroom sycophant in a moment of madness and/or high reprieve. "It looks dumb anyhow!"

"*What* did you say?" asks the teacher. "What did *you* say?"

The boy smiles.

"Repeat what you just said," Miss Daftly demands, looking at him from around the crumpled newspapers.

The boy continues smiling.

General unrest develops. Children begin to poke at one another. Someone says, "Let's take a vote." There is much giggling. Someone begins to whimper. It is Marcia. "Billy hit me *again!*" she wails.

The door opens. It is Tommy. He has returned.

With the last gasp of a dying duck, Miss Daftly calls out, "Bring me *that string!*"

Tommy steadfastly walks toward his teacher and says "Miss Green says to tell you that she don't gots any string."

Possibly the most basic of tenets in the establishment of classroom control is P&O, or the ability to *plan and to organize*.

For some of the more fortunate of teachers, this presents little in the way of a problem, for they learned to plan and to organize very early in their lives, and the transfer of this ability into the classroom is a smooth and easy operation.

Other teachers represent the late bloomers or those who learned P&O through experiences in trial and error.

"I used to spin my wheels," one teacher said. "By the time I had found the materials I had misplaced, my students were completely out of control!"

Another commented, "I used to gravitate toward the easiest way of doing things in my salad years, or my green years, of teaching. It seemed to me then that it would be far more simple to 'teach off the top of my head' and to 'play it by ear.' It took experience to teach me that my concept of *easy* was exhausting in its haphazardness, and demoralizing in its ineffectiveness. After I had begun to invest my time in planning and organizing, I realized that the sum total of my time thus spent would never exceed the time I had previously lost in frustration!"

Some teachers may ask, "How do you *do* it? I could *never* plan. I could *never* organize. I have always envied teachers who could."

Among such disorganized teachers, there is a somewhat generalized misconception that the ability to plan and to organize is inbred among the select few. One would be led to believe through their abject defeatism that P&O is joined by treaty with the science of genetics.

The organized teacher, on the other hand, will say, "Planning and organizing takes a high degree of stick-to-itiveness, plus a firm dedication to the premise that there *must be* and *can be* an easier way. The easier way can never be considered effortless. It takes mental concentration and muscle grease, but, when you see the results, you become addicted to the new and smoother running classroom operation!"

Even though some teachers have been teaching for years, they still perpetuate the practice of writing everything down on paper. "My lesson plans are not so elaborate as they once were," a teacher commented. "I find it supportive to look at my written notations just to check myself out. If I plan well, I will know what materials I will need; if I organize well, I will know where to find them."

The important concept of P&O can be understood as it relates to classroom control only when it is tried for its effectiveness and then weighed in terms of teaching economy. Former classroom failures in control can become acceptable when they provide the means for comparison and the reasons for striving.

The child who once said that his teacher was suffering from "battle-fatigue" was speaking the unvarnished truth. Disorganization and lack of planning can do nothing for a teacher except to give him a frenzied type of existence and a continual look of harassment.

When P&O becomes a habit, it will no longer become necessary to *plan*-to-organize, no more than it will become necessary to *organize*-to-plan. A routine that becomes easy, *does it!*

5 Contentment Is a Pretty Room

It is a truism that a warm greeting begets a warm response. Anything contrary to this thinking on the first day of school would be a massive blunder. At the outset, therefore, the new teacher and the new classroom become, by necessity, *that person* and *that place* toward which all children, singularly and collectively, find themselves becoming favorably disposed.

A pleasantly arranged room environment with a variety of interesting and thought-provoking areas can do much to assure one's students that they are welcome and, what is more important, that *each one of them* has been expected.

This can do more for a teacher than any number of articulated promises that school is going to be a happy place and that they are really going to like that man or woman who stands above them at front center.

The initial concept for development of the room's environment as well as its final execution, take place in the weeks or days that precede the opening of school. It is at this time when information is gained relative to policies and procedures, school rules, and curriculum patterns, and at this time when informal conferences are held with former teachers, and at this time when cumulative records are read, and at this time when books and materials are obtained and set out or stored in a functional manner, and finally, it is at this time when the arranged room environment is created in terms both of function and of aesthetic qualities.

The following represents a partial check list for the establishment of the arranged room environment:

1. Lighting: The source of light and its positive potential for maximum utilization in terms of function and/or comfort in a learning setting are of initial portentous significance.

Diminishing the probability of glare on blackboards, as well as diminishing the probability that children look directly into the light source from windows, would be checking points for arranging the angle of moveable desks.

2. Floor plan: Moveable desks, tables, bookshelves, and other standard types of school equipment will allow for the creation of a functionally designed floor plan. Consideration should be given to ensuring easy passageways in and out of the classroom with accessibility to doorways, blackboards, clothes closets, paper supplies, books, and interest centers for extra-time activities.

3. Basic color* scheme: The formation of a basic color scheme in terms of design unity would preclude the arbitrary selection of colored papers for displays, e.g., construction paper, tonal paper, corrugated paper, etc.

Generally it can be stated that, if a room is sunny, cool colors should be used; if the room is cool, warm colors should be used; if the room is small, cool colors will achieve a feeling of spaciousness; if the room is large, warm colors will achieve a feeling of less spaciousness.

For unity as well as for asethetic reasons, color selections should not include more than three colors. For example, if a

---

* For additional information relating to color and color theory, mounting and matting, bulletin-board arrangements, as well as detailed descriptions of art terms, materials, tools, and processes in the development of classroom art programs, see Katherine C. LaMancusa, *Source Book for Art Teachers* (Scranton, Pennsylvania: International Textbook Company, 1965).

warm-color harmony included the colors orange and red-orange, an accent color in the cool range, such as blue, could be effectively used. Conversely, if a cool color scheme is to be used, such as a combination of blue and blue-green, an accenting color of orange could be used.

The psychology of color is of portentous significance in the establishment of a room environment and the subsequent establishment of classroom control. In a teacher's first arranged room environment, particularly when he is dealing with qualitative and quantitative personality factors in the unknown, it would be well to select basic color schemes that work *toward* classroom control, and not work *against* it. It is important for the teacher to understand, for example, that the cool colors such as the blues and the greens tend to bring about feelings of tranquility and calm, while the warm colors tend to bring about feelings of excitement and stimulation. Witness, for example, the greens that are used on the walls in surgery rooms in hospitals, as well as the greens that are worn by attending doctors and nurses. On the other hand, witness the reds and the oranges that are used at carnivals and at circuses!

When qualitative and quantitative factors relative to control are unknown, specifically in the personality makeup of one's class, as well as in the numbers thereof, it would be wise to select dominant color schemes in the cool range and leave the warmer hues for a later date when more data are gathered and/or when the control factor is more thoroughly established in the classroom.

4. Bulletin boards and other related areas: This would involve, by necessity, the collection of all materials which would be used for purposes of display in the two-dimensional bulletin-board areas, as well as extended areas of related three-dimensional realia. The mounting and matting of all visual display

material would follow the established color scheme within the classroom. Realia should be authentic and interesting, providing for experiences in touching, feeling, and/or close inspection. Pertinent material in chart form, relating to monitorships, numerical concepts, and social studies, for example, should be provided and planned in terms of utilizing wall space. Included for consideration should be science tables, library shelves or tables, and extra-time activity centers (which could take the form of art tables, for example, with related tools and materials).

A careful inventory of students' interests and capabilities relative to periodicals and publications, for reading as well as for display, would be a necessity! For example, a child with a known interest in rock formations should have, if possible, a collection of interesting rocks displayed for him at the science table, as well as related reading materials available for him at the library table or shelves. It is important that this reading material reach him not only in terms of interest, but in terms of his own personal level of competency and/or ability in reading.

In this frame of reference, the so-called problem child can find a positive relating factor in his new room and with his new teacher when his interests and needs have been thoroughly met.

Bringing a touch of magic into the classroom in terms of flowers and plants, birds and fish, will provide, as well, opportunities for coveted monitorships in their care and maintenance.

The possiblities for incidental learnings in art appreciation and/or general perceptual awareness can be fostered with the placement of fine pieces of sculpture, well designed vases, and interesting and provocative mobiles, for example. Color reproductions of fine paintings and prints, as well as graphic representations of other fine art forms, may be purchased inexpensively from many sources. One of the many vendors of art reproductions is: Penn Prints, William Penn Publishing Corporation, 221 Park Avenue South, New York 3, New York.

5. Materials: Books such as basic texts and supplementary texts and materials such as pencils, crayons, erasers, and pens should be obtained from book depositories and supply centers within the school.

A calculated counting of heads, in terms of needed materials, is necessary, and it is always strongly advisable to obtain *extras* in order to allow for human error or the unexpected new child.

It is a time-saving device, as well as a transitional device, to place crayons, *sharpened pencils,* and certain common publications such as music books, *inside the desks.* Other specific materials and books which relate specifically to individuals and their grouping could be distributed at a later date when the students meet with the teacher for their first lesson.

Needed extra materials such as supplies of writing papers can be placed in designated locations so that students may develop a sense of self-direction. Reserve supplies of books and materials should be stacked in the teacher's *personal* supply cabinets.

6. Seating: Often teachers prefer to allow the children to select their own desks and thereby form their own seating arrangement. Quite obviously this presents a risk in terms of control. But the *reasonableness* of this initial teacher gesture will do much to create an image of being a *nice person.* Teachers may protect themselves by saying, "Yes, you may sit where you wish, and I will allow you to sit there for the rest of the semester—provided, of course, that you can work effectively there. If, as the semester progresses, it be-

comes apparent to me that you cannot work *well* where you are now seated, then it will become necessary for me to move you to another desk. Is that agreeable and understood?"

In order to facilitate familiarity, in attaching the name to the face of students, some teachers tape the children's names to their desks. These, of course, have already been lettered and *are ready for distribution.* The lettered names always give the individual child a decided boost in terms of his ego. *His* teacher really expected *him,* and, look, *his* teacher even *spelled his name correctly!*

An alternate method, and most assuredly a firmer controlling method, is the preplanned, teacher-designed seating arrangement. In this method the teacher has not only anticipated, but has geographically divided potential trouble areas. It is quite true that pals seldom work efficiently when seated in close proximity, nor do children with hostilities toward one another.

Other factors for positive preplanning consideration are: a scattering of girls among a thick cluster of boys and, conversely, a scattering of boys among a thick cluster of girls; the gregarious and talkative children scattered among the withdrawn and quiet and a calculated placement of the withdrawn and quiet among the gregarious and talkative groupings; and the children with poor work habits scattered among the children with good work habits.

The planned seating arrangement also makes provision for the children with visual and hearing impairments without necessarily calling undue attention to their handicap and the need to place them near the front of the room.

In the arranged seating plan, also, there is the opportunity for the teacher to affix children's names to their desks before they arrive in the classroom on the first day.

Teachers have said that an arranged room environment works positively in the establishment and maintenance of control. "When I take down my room environment, even for one day, the control factor is more difficult," one teacher said. "Where there are interesting displays within a child's range of vision, it gives his eyes something on which to light and his mind something on which to cogitate."

A teacher's room is his calling card. It either says, "Come in, I have been expecting you!" Or it says, "Good grief! another school year has begun."

Whatever it says by way of greeting, a teacher may be assured that his students will answer in kind. They will, on that important first day of school, be either alert and cooperative in the warmth of promised expectations or apathetic and negative in the greyed atmosphere of promised disconcern.

It would be the wise teacher indeed who, on the first day of school, would open the door with a smile and then stay unobtrusively in the background in order to allow his students a period of time in which to relate to their new teacher, new classroom, and its arranged environment. The teacher would answer questions now and again, but on a one-to-one basis, and with a soft voice that would barely penetrate the warp and the weft of the delicate fabric of beginning right.

6 Who Will Clean Our Lovely Snake Cage?

It would be difficult to deny the importance of an attractively arranged room environment, and teachers who ascribe to this thinking would find it commensurately difficult to deny the importance of maintenance in terms of housekeeping.

An orderly, well-stated classroom will give a child pride in his environment, and, when that child is permitted to contribute to its upkeep, he will relate to it with a higher degree of meaningfulness.

Keeping crayon boxes in order, washing out paint jars and brushes, sorting and stacking books, and emptying pencil sharpeners are but a few of the monitorships that children will joyfully accept in terms of shared responsibilities.

These teacher-designed activities may be considered experiences which will contribute to the education of the whole child. Transfers in learning in areas of responsibility and dependability may well reach fruition in the classroom and then carry over into the home as well. In assuming his fair share of home responsibilities, a child's systematic endeavor to keep his room in order may give him, perhaps for the first time, a real sense of being a contributing member of his own household.

Classroom monitorships in housekeeping tasks can be teacher assigned, rotated, or may be casually offered as they arise from need. For example, a teacher might look at a disorderly pile of papers and say, "Isn't it a shame that we can't keep that pile of papers looking neat? I wonder if there is someone who will assume the responsibility for keeping our paper in order?"

The teacher might make the observation, "We really need a responsible person who will check our pencil sharpener from time to time to see if it needs emptying. It will have to be someone who is dependable and reliable, for I would not like to think that I would have to remind him, in order to get the job done."

Constant praise when a job is done well and continued praise when a job is done independently are the kinds of reinforcements that are needed in order to establish standards for effective routine. When a teacher is both lavish and constant with his praise, he will find that he is doing more praising than reminding. It is that simple. At the same time, running concurrently with this concept of whole-child education, is the very real truism that such monitorships can lead back directly to the teacher as well as to the child. When a teacher's time and energies are saved, he has more time to devote to productive endeavors, specifically to the depth teaching of his students.

Monitorships give children a composite of positive feelings including a sense of well-being, security, and importance. It is a round-robin thought process for a child when he can say, "All is well in my classroom, and all will continue to go well. I have my job to do, and they have theirs; it will benefit me and them alike, because my teacher cares. And because my teacher cares, all is well in my classroom, and all will continue to go well—"

The orderliness of the classroom in terms of its maintenance in the arranged room environment, can become a natural relating factor toward the orderliness of conduct in the maintenance of desired standards for control, for this, too, is an individual and cooperative endeavor.

The following represents a partial listing of possibilities for monitorships within the classroom setting:

1. Time monitor: Responsible for making announcements relative to time for clean-up, for recess, for lunch, etc.

2. Closet monitor: Responsible for the orderliness of the clothes closet including follow-through in seeing that children hang up clothes, keep rain boots secured together with clothespins, and that wearing apparel is labeled with names, etc.

3. Wastepaper monitor: Responsible for emptying waste paper into large trashcans when room baskets are full.

4. Errand monitor: Responsible for carrying all messages to the office and to other classrooms.

5. Phonograph monitor: Responsible for keeping records in order and for operating phonograph.

6. Projector and film monitor: Responsible for obtaining projector and screen, threading projector, showing film, re-winding film, and taking projector back to audiovisual room.

7. Bird-animal-fish monitor: Responsible for cleaning cages or aquariums and for feeding birds, animals, or fish.

8. Plant monitor: Responsible for the watering and feeding of plants.

9. Flower monitor: Responsible for selecting vase, arranging, changing water, and discarding old flowers.

10. Floor monitor: Responsible for seeing that papers are picked up from the floor.

11. Crayon monitor: Responsible for the distribution of needed crayons and for the collection of crayons that have been left on the floor.

12. Pencil monitor: Responsible for the distribution of pen-

cils, including the collection of pencils which have been left on the floor.

13. Pencil sharpener monitor: Responsible for the cleaning of pencil shavings from the sharpener.

14. Paper monitor: Responsible for keeping paper supply stocked and in order.

15. Workbook monitor: Responsible for the collecting and returning of workbooks.

16. Corrected papers monitor: Responsible for passing back all corrected papers.

17. Science table monitor: Responsible for keeping science table in order and for displaying new materials and equipment.

18. Library table monitor: Responsible for keeping library table in order, stacking books properly, and displaying new books.

19. Art table monitor: Responsible for keeping tools clean and in good working order; restocking paper, mixing paints, and providing needed materials for specific processes.

20. Dusting monitor: Responsible for all dusting in the classroom.

21. Milk monitor: Responsible for obtaining milk from central depository and distributing milk and straws.

22. Cracker monitor: Responsible for ordering and distributing crackers in milk program.

23. Ball monitor: Responsible for distribution of balls, jump ropes, and other equipment; for maintenance, proper use, and return.

24. Window monitor: Check room temperature; open and close windows in classroom.

25. Window shades monitor: Responsible for adjusting shades.

26. Light monitor: Responsible for switching lights on and off when necessary.

27. Door monitor: Responsible for opening and closing of all classroom doors when necessary.

28. Blackboard monitor: Responsible for erasing boards when necessary.

29. Blackboard eraser monitor: Responsible for cleaning erasers.

30. Desk monitor: Responsible for inspections in the maintenance of neat desks.

31. Bulletin board and display monitor: Responsible for taking down bulletin board and display materials, storing pictures, pins, and realia in proper files or cabinets.

32. Host monitor: Responsible for greeting visitors to the classroom; also responsible for orientation of all new students to school and classroom.

33. Telephone monitor: Responsible for answering the telephone when the teacher is unable to do so.

34. Roll monitor: Responsible for daily roll taking.

35. Flag monitor: Responsible for flag saluting exercises.

36. Rainy day monitor: Responsible for obtaining, distributing, and collecting games for indoor activities during days of rain and other types of inclement weather.

7 The Broken-Crayon Monitor

I shall never forget Joey, no more than I shall ever forget the way he looked on that morning in midsemester, when his mother brought him into my second grade classroom. I had said to him, "We need a new boy in our classroom, Joey. The boys will be happy to see you."

He was not impressed. Indeed it appeared as if he had not heard me at all. He continued looking down at his feet.

Poor Joey, I thought. He was anything but a boy's concept of a regular guy. Inordinately short and fat, with hair slicked down so that it appeared to be glued to his head, save for a cowlick that stuck up in back like a geyser, he gave no assurance that he either wanted to be a boy in my class or that the children in the class would accept him. His enormous blue eyes were vacuous in expression, glasslike and pink lined from crying. On both sides of his small button nose, his cheeks looked like ripe halved apples. His mouth hung flaccidly opened with his tongue protruding like a cork. As I observed him further, I noted that he did not walk, he ambled. He did not stand, he leaned. He did not sit, he slumped. When I asked him if I pronounced his last name correctly, he answered, "Yeth."

With all of that, Joey had to lisp, too!

His mother took my arm and together we walked to a corner of the room. "He is not a good student," she said. "I am afraid that he doesn't like school. He has asthma and he's been absent a great deal. I have tried to help him to catch up in his work, but he has little energy." She shrugged her shoulders hopelessly, "Sometimes, I confess, I just don't know what to do."

I nodded. "I understand."

"But he's a good boy. So sweet and thoughtful. He doesn't understand it when he can't breathe, sometimes, at night. He doesn't sleep. We can't send him to school when he has been ill. You understand?"

"Of course."

"It's not just that. He's not like other boys his age, and he knows it. He hasn't the capacity to run and play. It's made him shy, and almost—almost friendless."

"Will he cry when you leave him today?" I asked.

"Possibly. I don't know."

"Well, let's hope that he doesn't," I said.

"I'll do more than that," she said.

Joey's mouth began to quiver when his mother left and I said to him quickly, "We are going to have to find a job for you."

He stared at me uncomprehendingly.

"Did you have a job in your other school?"

He shook his head.

"Do you know what a monitor is, Joey?"

Yes, he knew. He nodded.

"Would you like to be a monitor, Joey?"

"I dunno. I can't read very good."

"You don't have to read in order to be a monitor."

"You hafta path out thoeth paperth."

"No you don't. There are other kinds of jobs."

He leaned forward on my desk and cupped his chin in his hands. "What other kindth are there?"

"There's a door monitor, a milk monitor, a cracker monitor. . . ."

"OK."

"OK what?"

"I'll be one of thoeth."

"I'm afraid you can't be one of those, Joey," I said, "but I will find another job for you."

"Why can't I be one of thoeth?"

"Because, Joey, those jobs belong to other children. We'll find a nice job for you."

"Like what kind?"

"Let me see." I thought for a while. What was left? In a classroom of forty children, a teacher might well find herself jobbed out. What *was* left?

"Have you thought of anything?" he asked.

"No, but there must be something." I leaned down to pick up a broken crayon from the floor and then laid it on my desk.

"Have you got one of thoeth?"

"One of what?"

"A broken-crayon monitor?"

"A broken-crayon monitor?"

"Yeth."

"No, I haven't. But, it sounds like a good job."

He nodded. "Do I get it?"

"Yes, indeed. That will be your job, Joey. And, a very good job it will be. When crayons are dropped on the floor, they often get stepped on. Even the custodian has complained. Yes, Joey. That will be your job. You will pick up broken crayons from the floor."

And so it was that Joey became our broken-crayon monitor. At first he would only collect the small broken crayons on which the children had stepped. Later, he was not so discriminate. He picked up *all* crayons that were lying on the floor. These would include new and whole crayons as well as the old and broken ones. He never threw any of them away but, instead, pushed them inside his own desk. In time, he put them into a small box, and later he went a step further. He brought a large manila envelope from home and labeled it, "JUMK." Into the "Jumk Envelope" went the small unusable crayons, while the larger and usable ones were contained in his box.

One day, during a reading lesson with a small group of children, I heard voices coming from the back of the room. Two children were shouting at each other. One was Joey.

"Come on, Joey, that's mine. I was going to pick it up," a child said.

"It was on the *floor*," Joey protested.

From this altercation, came some ground rules for Joey's job. It was decided that if a child dropped his crayon, he would have to pick it up immediately; otherwise Joey could collect it. From that moment on, most children would hastily pick up their crayons for fear that Joey would approach with his box.

The next stage of development in the broken-crayon monitorship came as a natural outgrowth of Joey's vast supplies of crayons. Whenever children needed a crayon of a particular color, they would approach Joey's desk and ask him for one. Joey was discriminating with his supplies. If he felt that there was a dearth of blacks for example, he would not be above breaking a crayon in half before he handed it to the child.

He was aware of who the irresponsible children were or those who constantly asked for the same color of crayon day after day. "I gave you a red yesterday," he would say.

"I know Joey, But I lost it."

"I don't have many redth," he would say as he snapped a crayon in half.

I was never fully aware of its happening. But it *did* happen. Joey became a most popular child. The broken-crayon monitorship (in the manner in which Joey had developed it) became a prestige position. The children were perceptive enough to realize that if they won the friendship of Joey, "the keeper of the crayons," he would not be above allowing his finger to slip a bit off dead center when he snapped a crayon in half. Why, there was no telling how many good "redth" one might accrue! There were even those who began to ask when they, too, might become broken-crayon monitors. "How come Joey always gets to do it?" they would ask.

It was about this time that I evaluated my broken-crayon monitor in every phase of his development. It seemed to me that he was becoming less chubby and more lean. The vacuous expression had disappeared, and his absences became less and less frequent. He was even playing kickball with the boys on the field. "Come on, Joey," they would shout to him as he lapped the bases. "Come on, Joey, run, run, run! Atta boy, Joey. Atta boy!"

Joey had made the adjustment. Yet, he had done more than that. He had gained status, friends, academic achievement, and even his health had improved.

It made me think all over again of that frightened little boy who leaned on my desk, lisping and prescribing his own formula for success. "Have you got one of thoeth?"

"One of what?" I had asked.

"A broken-crayon monitor?"

8 Now Enter Billy Bully

The Billy Bullies of the teaching world need no introduction. If there is a Billy Bully in the student body the teacher who has him need wear no name tag.

The exploits of the Billy Bullies in and out of the classroom have been chronicled in fat cumulative record folders, and their names have been bandied about in teachers' lounges over gallons of tepid coffee and cartons of cigarettes.

It does a teacher little good to pound his chest and to cast his eyes skyward when an illustrious name is attached to his classroom roster. "Why *me?*" or "What have I done to deserve *this?*" are common entreaties.

To what avail are these pleas, which are ill accepted, when the plain statistical facts of the teaching life would indicate that there are five Billy Bullies to every four and one-half teachers!

The Billy Bullies of the teaching milieu are manifold and diverse. They are the same children that teachers pull down from cyclone fences and the same children that cut off little girls' braids and, indeed, the same children who hide under bus seats when a teacher is counting students' noses after a field trip on a submarine.

How does a teacher prepare himself for a Billy Bully, particularly when such a child is expected to appear in his classroom on the first day of a new semester?

The following procedural steps in the care and handling of Billy Bullies have been tested in classroom proving grounds:

1. Avoid Panic: An ounce of prevention is truly worth a pound of cure! Assume the attitude that *worry will not change the impending situation, but positive and deliberate effort will.*

2. Gather Data: Read his cumulative record folder and assess his comprehensive social ·pattern as well as his comprehensive academic record. Arrange informal conferences with his former teachers as well as with the school counselor (if he has been receiving counseling services). Where do his strengths lie; his weaknesses? What health impairments might contribute to his negative social behavior? How long has it been since he has had a physical examination, an eye test, or a hearing test? If it appears that he has not had a physical examination for a long period of time, arrange a conference with the school nurse.

A teacher who once spoke of a child as being wholly "impossible" related this story: "Jimmy baffled me. If I said, 'Do not open that side door,' he would open it! If I said, Walk quietly down the hall,' he would run!

"When I spoke to his former teacher about his behavior, she said, 'Jimmy? Why, he was a lovely child in *my* classroom.'

" 'He must be deaf,' I said to myself. Then, I said out loud, 'Maybe he *is!*'

"When I got back into the classroom, I tested my hypothesis. 'Jimmy,' I said. There was no response. He did not even look up at me.

"A hearing test was arranged for him and later it was discovered that he had a severe hearing loss in the low range of sounds. His former teacher had a high voice. He had heard her. My voice was low. He had never really heard me ever since he had been in my classroom!

"When he started wearing his hearing aid, both his problems and my problems disappeared. He *was* a lovely child."

Another teacher related the story of a fourth grade problem child who could not read. She observed that he squinted when he looked at the blackboard and held his book very close to his eyes. She observed further that his eyes had never been tested, so she requested a conference with the school nurse. A Snellen Eye Test revealed that the boy should seek further testing with an ophthamologist. Thereafter, glasses were prescribed. In a short time the child traveled from first grade reading ability to fourth. There was never any recurrence of social or academic failures. The child said, "Now that I have my glasses, I can see the eyes on people in the movies."

3. Think Positively: Keep the mind open and allow yourself the pleasure of hopeful thought projection in meeting a challenge head-on. Repeat often, "*I* will reach Billy Bully. I *will* reach him."

4. Plan and Do: In setting up the arranged room environment, plan for specific displays, books, and/or realia which would appeal to Billy's interests.

For example, a teacher once paid twelve dollars for a sturdy second-hand typewriter simply because she knew *her* Billy Bully had a burning desire to learn to type. Billy had developed this interest rather incidentally. He had been "bounced" out of his former classrooms and had been sent to the office quite often. He would pass his time there, in total mesmerization, watching the secretary typing letters.

The teacher said later, after Billy was well in tow, "Yes, I paid twelve dollars for that typewriter, and I was never remuneratively reimbursed. However, in the critical early period of establishing working relationships, and in the months that followed, I was reimbursed in a way that money could not buy!"

5. Operational Strategy: Avoid coming on too strong when

Billy enters the classroom. It is a tactical error to point one's finger at Billy and say, "In this room, I'm the boss, and don't you ever forget it!" A pox on that approach. He has heard it before!

Although you may have had altercations with Billy in the past relating to yard behavior and hallway running, *at this time* it is *imperative* that you convey the impression that all is forgotten and all is forgiven. In other words, develop a bad memory which is clinically induced.

It is better, in terms of approach, to smile a pleasant greeting and follow this with a few pointed comments relating to the "interesting displays." This will suffice for the initial period of "baiting."

6. Planned Seating: Intensive planning relating to seating is essential. Children's names should be lettered and adhered to desks with tape before they arrive on the first day. Surround Billy with children who are conscientious and who consistently display good working habits. Box him in with serenity and calm.

7. Building Ego: Seek out that first opportunity to compliment Billy on some seemingly mundane act, which is either consciously or unconsciously performed.

For example, even if he is late in arriving, overlook this indiscretion and say, "I want to thank you Billy, for closing that door so quietly. It is always a pleasure for a teacher to know that there are considerate children in his class. Sometimes students forget and slam the doors. However, *you* Billy, were considerate. Thank you."

Billy is now "hooked," and all that remains is the "catch."

8. Skilled Catching: During the distribution or offering of monitorships, a particularly coveted and custom-designed job should be saved for Billy. For example, trading on the known

fact that Billy is interested in typewriters, a teacher might say, "We need a monitor for a very important job—a typewriter monitor. Oh dear, so many hands! Billy Bully, I understand that you are interested in learning to type. Are you? Very well, then, I shall teach you to type. Of course, I will do it in your extra time *when you have finished all of your classroom assignments.* Until then, it will be your responsibility to take the cover off the typewriter every morning and to keep a fresh supply of typewriter paper at the table. When you learn how to type, you may teach other students. This is an important job Billy. It will need constant attention. That typewriter is *your* responsibility. It will mean that you will have to finish your work on time, learn to type, and teach others. Do you still want the job, Billy? You do? Very well then, Billy Bully is our typewriter monitor."

Billy is caught. The catch has been made!

9. Follow Through: As Billy assumes this monitorship the teacher will continually remind him that he was chosen because of his reliability and conscientiousness. Remember that positive behavior will come most efficaciously from assuming that *expectations have already been met.* It is never, "I expect you to *be*—because you have this job," but rather, "You have this job, because you *are*—"

Remember also, that the Billy Bullies are starved for acceptance and praise and will soak up compliments like a dry sponge. Keep the compliments coming at regular intervals.

Continue to provide fresh and exciting surprises for Billy. It will never be enough to make him the typewriter monitor and then to forget about it. Children have short interest spans generally, and most experiences will grow old and wither on the vine without the nourishment of additives. Teach Billy how to change a typewriter ribbon. Provide new kinds of ribbons such as red and black, or brown ones, for his experimentation. Teach him how to use carbon paper. Provide carbon in different colors.

Above all, show him that you really *care* about him and that you are really interested in knowing how he is getting along. If he is absent or ill, have the children make some get-well cards for him and send them in the mail. Add a note from yourself and tell him how much he is missed and how much you hope for his speedy recovery.

10. Provide Challenges: Send him off to the library with a specific assignment relative to the historical development of the typing machine. Allow him the opportunity to deliver his report orally to the class. Consort with other teachers so that Billy may be allowed to be a guest lecturer in other classrooms, particularly in the awesome upper grades.

11. Salvaging Self-Respect: Give him opportunities to erase his former image. If he spent the major portion of his previous semester warming the bench in the office, allow him to deliver messages to the principal (as a trusted and respected classroom citizen). Or, send him to the office so that he can show the principal a particularly fine piece of work he has done. Send along a note saying, "I thought you would like to know of Billy's splendid progress. He has made such a fine record."

Granted that the Billy Bullies will find their moments of plateau and/or retrogression. Treat these as they arise, fairly and squarely. Not with a big fuss, but with the philosophy that tomorrow will be another day and that everyone gets up on the wrong side of his bed once in a while. It is important, however, that continued retrogression be checked: it is important for Billy, and it is important in terms of unified classroom control.

Such instances can be treated clinically and on a businesslike basis. "Well Billy, since you did not finish your work today, you will have to remain after school in order to finish it." That's all that needs to be said. Say it with a smile that will show that it is nothing personal—but plainly the facts of life in a slice of living.

At the same time, and concurrent with setting down limitations, continue compliments when he evidences positive behavior—and continue providing those surprises.

A seasoned teacher said of her particular Billy Bully, "I have never had a child like him before or since. He stayed after school frequently because I nailed him every time he stepped out of line. I was consistent and unyielding in my persistence toward behavioral standards. However, in the end, on the last moment of that last day of school, when he leaned on my desk to say good-bye to me—he found he could not. Tears welled in his eyes, and ran down his cheeks. Finally he gasped, "I'll never forget you. You were the best teacher I ever had."

When teachers demonstrate that they really *care* about a child and his behavior, they are in effect demonstrating that they love that child. This kind of love need not be articulated. A child knows and understands.

9 We Do Not Throw Rocks at the Teacher!

Standards for classroom conduct cannot and do not come from a vacuum. They arise from a stated need when they are germinated in the minds of children. They are articulated and discussed under the guidance of the teacher, who lists them by writing them on the board and later transfers them to a chart.

There are some teachers who allow their classrooms to malfunction until the time becomes propitious to seek out a solution for the establishment of a more favorable climate for study. The discussions in the realm of standards for behavior usually follow a child's comment that the room is too noisy for study.

"Then, what shall we do about it?" a teacher might ask his students.

Other teachers, who are less experienced in this type of permissiveness, would nip the problem in the bud very early in the first week of school. This type of teacher might ask, "How shall we act in our classroom so that everyone may work well?"

When a teacher allows his students to formulate their own suggestions, he is at the same time assured that his students understand with clarity that he is not inflicting *his will over theirs*. Rather, it is they, themselves, who are establishing their own rules for acceptable classroom behavior. *This is most important.*

Experienced teachers in the field will attest to the fact that children will grind very fine their expectations for conduct. "It is as though they are inflicting these rules on the other fellow, not themselves," a teacher once observed.

Educators believe that, as the children offer their suggestions, it is important for the teacher to allow them to rephrase offerings in order that the blackboard listing does not have an overwhelmingly negative connotation. For example, "Don't talk when the teacher is talking," might be rephrased as, "We listen when the teacher is talking to us."

No teacher would attempt to write every suggestion on the board. In helping children to be discriminate and selective a teacher might say, "That's a good point, but do you really think it is necessary to list that one on the board? Not many students who are as grown up and responsible as you would do that sort of thing. Would they?"

On the other hand, a teacher might comment, "That is an important point. I am glad that we thought about that one."

When overlapping occurs, a comment might refine thinking. "Didn't John say the same thing in the second suggestion? Let's read it and see."

When a full listing of classroom standards is on the board and the teacher is satisfied that every area for concern is covered, a discussion might follow which would relate to the *reasonableness* of the suggestions.

"I think you have made an excellent listing," the teacher might say. "Have we forgotten something? Is there anything further that you would like to add? Very well then, is it agreed among us that we will live up to these standards for classroom conduct? Let me see how many of you think you can?"

As the waving hands indicate agreement, the teacher announces that the standards will be printed in chart form and will be hung on the wall, "so that we can all see them and remember them."

A typical *Room-Standards Chart* might contain the following:

1. We raise our hands before talking.
2. We work quietly at our desks.
3. We avoid talking when it is not necessary.
4. We listen when the teacher is talking to us.
5. We wait until a person has finished talking before we say something.
6. We walk in the room at all times.
7. We sharpen our pencils only at recess time.
8. We are courteous and considerate of others.
9. We make good use of our extra time.

When the Room-Standards Chart is hung prominently in the classroom, a teacher may use it as a point of reference when a child displays deviant behavior. "Which room standard did you *forget?*" the teacher might ask.

The word "forget" is used in order to soften the reprimand and to provide the child with a respectable alternative.

In the adjustment period that lies ahead, it is important that the teacher remember not to count an infringement of the rules as a personal affront but rather as an unfortunate lapse of memory, the result of which distressed and disturbed the entire class. It is not "I"; it is "we."

In these instances, a teacher might say, "John, *we* are trying to study in this reading group. *We* will have to stop now, because your talking is distracting our thinking. Which room standard did you forget?"

In the weeks that follow, the teacher is both *persistent and consistent.* These are the two key words toward ultimate success!

In spite of the weariness and tedium of not allowing the small things go by unnoticed, it is the wise teacher who will *keep at it.*

By way of illustration, a teacher once got into her car in order to intercept a child on his way home. He had slipped out of the classroom unnoticed, even though he was supposed to stay after school. This is the degree of persistency and consistency that is needed, and not a smidgen less.

Although Emerson said, "A foolish consistency is the hobgoblin of little minds . . . ," one must remember that the word "foolish" cannot be tagged on, either by fact or fancy, to the important area of classroom control.

10 On Giving In for the Moment

In the uphill climb toward effectiveness in one's teaching role and for perfection in matters of control, there will be periods of retrogression and plateau which will bring with them feelings of self-doubt and failure. Assume that there is a line which is the shortest distance between the two points "chaos" and "control." Let it be said emphatically that the line is *not always* upward, slanting, and onward in the straight-tilted-diagonal manner, but is *often* upward, level, and backward in the jagged-straight-angular fashion.

When all that has been reinforced and gained appears to be slipping back to sea in a frightful undertow, it is best not to attempt to fight the elements. For the moment, it is enough to keep one's head above water and swim with the tide. In avoiding panic one conserves energy for that propitious time when one may swim home again and feel the support and comfort of solid operational ground.

Typically, in all school days and semesters, there will be those moments of little response and retention. It takes experience to know under what circumstances these situations occur, and it takes a philosophical approach to know what to do about them—specifically, to treat them lightly and go on striving toward reaching one's projected goals.

In Chapter 9, "We do not Throw Rocks at the Teacher," mention was made of the teacher who employed the word "forget" when referring to transgressions. This chapter will point up the reality of teacher understandings in the area of collective "forgetting." Moreover, it will be stated that a teacher's perception of this truism, in terms of application, will obviate continual reminding and continual articulation of, "How naughty you all are today!"

While this would appear to be a contradiction of the statement in Chapter 9 wherein it was said that "a teacher is both persistent and consistent" in the maintenance of room standards, there will nevertheless be those times when, in the light of tremendous odds, persistency and consistency would be sheer folly.

We know for example that a teacher must treat transgressions lightly in the first important days of establishing room standards. The teacher employs the word "forget." Beyond this, there are other factors for perusal. A classroom dominated by a high number of boys will need a teacher who understands that achieving success is a slow process. A class with an imbalance of boys over girls will quite possibly never achieve the kind of flawless control, in fruition, that would be possible if this imbalance were reversed with more girls than boys.

Along this same line of reasoning, control factors will be more difficult on a Friday than they would be on a Monday, just as control is more difficult to maintain in the afternoons than in the mornings. Child fatigue and perhaps teacher fatigue have a lot to do with this statement of factual reality. Control factors will always appear more difficult if the teacher is tired or distressed over some personal matter. And control factors will appear more difficult for the teacher if he dislikes, or feels insecure in, a specific subject area. Class make-up, with a high percentage of children from broken homes, will contribute to difficult control, just as will a high percentage of children who live in apartment houses, for lack of feelings of security and lack of space in which to run and play are all contributing factors. Each must be weighed and measured in terms of setting up realistic projected goals of classroom control.

Let us suppose for purposes of illustration that a young student teacher was attempting to get her second grade students under flawless control as they were lining up outside the school library after a long period of inactivity during a storytelling hour. Inexperience worked against this teacher initially, for she should have understood that these children had been inactive for too long a period of time and that her projections were unrealistic insofar as achieving a straight and quiet line, with children facing the front in a two-by-two fashion. However, she persisted in staying with her projected expectations.

"I am waiting for you to be quiet and to line up two-by-two," she said.

A cluster of boys at the end of the line hand linked their arms in trio fashion.

"John, Michael, and Larry! Please unlock your arms and take one partner."

The girls at the front of the line developed their own problems. It appeared that Jane who was at the head of the line, did not wish to take a partner. "Go away," said Jane, "I don't want a partner."

And then, in the middle of the line, a child's voice protested, "Someone's pushing." With that, the middle section pushed forward, thus scattering the girls outward in a fan fashion.

By this time the teacher was at the end of the line disengaging little boys' arms and sectioning boys off by twos. When she became aware that the middle section was pushing forward, she ran to the middle section and said firmly, "Get settled now, and stop that pushing!"

However, the girls at the front of the line, who had become dispersed in a fan fashion from the middle section's pushing, decided to retaliate and push back. Whereupon the middle section fell backwards. Two thirds of the class was now fanned out and dispersed.

"Stop this! Stop this!" the teacher shouted. "Take your partners again, get in line, and be quiet!"

By this time, there was general confusion as to where the partners were placed. "We were ahead of you," said Michael and Larry.

"You were not!" said John and Archibald.

"Children. Children. We shall not move until you are settled down and are quiet and are with your partners. *We will not move!*

"What seems to be the trouble?" asked the principal as he walked out of his office.

The teacher flushed pink. "I am trying to take my students back to their classroom," she said.

"Then *why* don't you take them?"

"They're so noisy and so disorderly. I am waiting for them to quiet down."

"Take them back to their classroom, my dear," said the principal, "it will *never* happen."

Fortunately for this young and inexperienced teacher, the principal arrived to relieve her from her impossible demands. Beyond this, the principal's directive illustrated that there *are* times when, in lieu of meeting expectations, one must act: *get on with it,* and settle for much less.

Tomorrow will be another day, enriched by one more day of experience. Everything that goes up, must come down. So, give in for the moment, and be glad!

11 A Pox on Him Who Finishes Too Fast!

Misconceptions are born easily but, unfortunately, die hard.

One of the prevailing errors in thought relating to "busy work" is that, if one piles it on the gifted child higher and deeper, it can then be called depth learning. In terms of classroom control, no one thought could be more devastating!

The gifted can present one of the more exasperating of positive situations for the classroom teacher. For, the mean for classroom achievement *is not their mean*. And, the mean for time allotments for finishing assignments *is not their mean*.

Albeit there are commonalities of basic bodies of knowledge and/or basic skills that must be taught to the gifted as well as to the child with average intelligence, an assignment given to them along these lines is like a mere thimble of water which is dropped into the vast Pacific. Their capacity for learning is like infinity, *endless*. They are the ones who finish their assignments a bit too fast for a teacher's comfort. Indeed, they gobble up fat assignments as if they were going out of style.

Unless a teacher provides for *real* and *meaningful* depth learnings, he will, in the parlance of the trade, find himself bolting for the door when the last bell rings. Depth learnings will necessitate extra planning; there is no shortcut to effective teaching. Related assignments, research problems, recreation reading, as well as experiences in experimentation and exploration with science equipment and art media are but a few suggestions for activities which would provide for easy transition when a child finishes his regular assignments.

Otherwise, the gifted children will always seem to approach the teacher when he has decided to sit down at his desk and, in the tradition of loafing, has planned for a brief period of "taking five."

They walk up to the teacher, toss their finished assignments on top of the desk and say, "What can I do now?"

Some neophytes, as well as some ineffectual teachers, might think that this problem can be solved on the spot. "Let's see, Archibald," a teacher may say, "why don't you sit down and write the squares of all uneven numbers up to one thousand?"

"All right," says Archibald. He walks to his desk, whips out his paper and pencil and begins his task.

The teacher smiles. "That will hold him," she says to herself. "That will hold Archie."

But lo, a few mintues later, Archibald is approaching the teacher once again. "Did you say the squares of all uneven numbers from one to one thousand?"

"Yes. That's what I said."

"Didn't you say last week that we should be conserving paper?"

"Yes—"

"Then why don't I save paper by giving them to you orally?"

"Orally?"

"Of course. It's quite simple—1, 9, 25, 49, 81, 121,—"

"That's enough, Archibald."

"I can go on."

"Yes, I am quite sure that you can."

"121, 169—"

"Archibald!"

Archibald stops.

"Why don't you go to the easel and paint?"

He demurs. "Something along the lines of an abstract-expressionistic statement?"

"That would be grand," the teacher says.

"Very well." Archibald walks away. Stops. Pivots about, and returns. "It is a pity we do not have a bunsen burner and some wax."

"Why is that, Archibald?"

"I was reading something about the wax-encaustic process that Leonardo attempted to revive in the High Renaissance. It intrigued me. I was thinking that if we had a bunsen burner, I could melt some wax in a can and color it with powdered tempera, and—"

"Look Archibald, why don't you *just* paint—*plain?* Like Michelangelo."

"Michelangelo painted with tempera mixed with eggs, on walls of fresh lime and gypsum," he smiles patronizingly.

"Is that right? Now Archibald, I am growing quite perturbed with this conversation. If you wish to paint, then paint as every other child paints in this school!"

"Tempera on paper?"

"Tempera on paper."

"Very well," says Archibald, "but I can assure you, the experience will be quite dull."

The area of *transition* is of importance not only in the teaching of the gifted but also in the teaching of *all children*, who will finish seat work with varying degrees of speed.

Chapter 9 discussed the importance of establishing room standards for behavior. One of the points listed on the room-standards Chart, specifically item #9, stated, "We make good use of our extra time."

Such a statement can be quite meaningless unless a teacher helps his students to understand what "good use of extra time," implies.

A discussion defining this concept will help to clarify what may appear for some children to be a highly abstract phrase.

By a child's interpretation, the statement may read, "doing what I wish."

By a teacher's interpretation, the statement may read, "keeping productively employed in meaningful endeavors."

In terms of control, the statement strongly says, "these are preventative procedures."

When a child finishes his work, if there is no direction for him in that block of time while others are still working, then there is apt to be a force of strong potential for disruption.

In some cases, it is enough to discuss extra-time activities on an oral basis; at other times, stronger reinforcement comes from the discussion-chart approach. Directions and their alternatives are listed on what some teachers call, an "Extra-Time Chart." Items included on this chart might read:

WHEN I AM FINISHED WITH MY WORK, I WILL:
1. Check finished work for possible errors.
2. Make up unfinished work.
3. Assume monitorship job.
4. Read books from the library table.
5. Work at science or art table.

When this chart is lettered and hung in a prominent spot for student referral, a teacher should help his students to understand that the chart is read most efficiently from the top to the bottom, and not in the reverse! Specifically, the chart says that when work is finished and checked for errors, unfinished work may then be completed. When this is done, then one will have time to assume his job as a monitor. When this is finished, he may elect to either read a book from the library table, work at the science table, or work at the art table.

No child can realistically complain that he has "nothing to do," when his avenues for direction are so clearly articulated and spelled out. Such planning of extra-time activities has been called, by this author at least, "dovetailing."

Another oft heard question which is directed at the classroom teacher is the one that queries, "I am finished now, *where do I put my work?*"

Quite obviously when a teacher has to stop what he is doing in order to direct a child in the deposition of a paper or workbook, he is expending needless energies. What is worse is that the interruption is distracting both the students and himself.

Along the lines of P&O, as well as in that important area of consistency and transition, a firm routine should be established. Labeled baskets, labeled boxes, or labeled trays will serve as utilitarian receptacles for papers and workbooks. They can be lined up next to each other on a shelf with captions reading: ARITHMETIC, SPELLING, HANDWRITING, SOCIAL STUDIES, etc. The use of duplicate receptacles, relative to groups and their numbers, is optional.

It is understood, of course, that finished assignments may be collected in diverse ways. For example, a spelling test which is given to a small group within the class, may be collected by a monitor within that group. Other common assignments, such as a handwriting exercise, might be more efficiently collected by instructing the students to pass their papers forward with one child collecting them across if seating arrangements would permit this. Transition and operational routine will be reinforced through specific monitorships for specific tasks of a unique nature, as stated in Chapter 6.

12 The Letter That Goes Home (Again)!

Every once in a while in a well-earned fit of pique, a teacher will plop himself at his desk and grab at his pen. His fine Zaner-Bloser hand will begin to scratch, scratch, scratch and jerk, jerk, jerk into what may be called the beginning stages of an emotional catharsis. The final gestures, in terms of tradition, are to slam down the pen, bang the sheet of writing paper into folded letter form, stick it into a manila envelope, lick it frothily, bang at the envelope, slap it down, and then, scrawl across the face of it, "Mr. and Mrs. Bully." At the lower left hand corner, the teacher adds, "Kindness of Billy Bully."

While the efficacy of writing a letter now and again cannot be denied under certain circumstances, the continued practice of chronicling negative behavior in letter form is a hopeless gesture.

Fewer letters to parents would become"lost" if the teacher granted the child the courtesy of knowing what was contained in the manila envelope. Ulcers are not uncommon among children. The known is far less threatening than the unknown. If the teacher deems it unwise to divulge the contents of the letter to the child, then, quite simply, the letter should never be written. A telephone call or an arranged conference would be more meaningful in terms of true communication.

Aside from this, letter writing can be dangerous, particularly if the teacher is unduly agitated and/or emotionally spent. An old Italian proverb states explicitly that one should "Think much, speak little, and write less."

Every problem child and every parent of a problem child is familiar with the type of letter which reads:

Dear Mr. and Mrs. Bully,

   I regret to inform you that Billy was most uncooperative today. It was necessary for me to speak to him, countless times, about his poor conduct. I would appreciate it if you would speak to him about his responsibilities as a good classroom citizen.

Very truly yours,
(Signed) Miss I. C. Redd

P.S. Would you kindly sign this letter and have Billy return it in the morning?

The parents of Billy Bully might well have enough of these letters to paper their living room. Billy's mother might sigh audibly when she is handed the familiar manila envelope, "Oh dear, here is another one!"

What is *really* gained by continually reminding parents that they have a "problem child" on their hands? Is this *news* to them? Not at all. They know it. They may not accept it, but they know it. And, even if they do accept it, what can they *do* about it? Obviously nothing. If there was anything that they could have done, they would have done it long ago. But, they are powerless. They need the same kind of guidance and understanding that Billy Bully needs. They need the combined resources that a school has to offer, including parent conferences, and then, perhaps, direction toward granting permission for counseling services.

Beyond the tedium of such letter writing, and the rather useless reinforcement of something that is already known, there is a more portentous reason for not continually writing and sending such missives. The psychology is *all* wrong. Not only does the letter bring about feelings of hostility which promote scenes between parent and parent and then eventually between parent and child, but also, and eventually, this hostility becomes directed toward the teacher and the school. Then all is lost!

"Look at that 'PS'!" a parent might say. "Sign this letter and have Billy return it in the morning! Doesn't that teacher think we teach our child to be trustworthy?"

Too often, teachers forget that a child *belongs* to his parents. However willing parents may appear to set Billy on a smooth and more acceptable course, it still hurts them deeply to realize that among all of the children in the classroom, it is *their* child who is the difficult one. How often they have wished that it was otherwise. How often they have searched themselves wondering what it was that they did that made Billy the way he is.

A wiser teacher would treat letter writing more positively. He might announce that he is prepared to write letters to parents *only* when students can exhibit commendable classroom behavior. The letter, then, would become something toward which all children will strive. Imagine, taking home a letter which would tell one's parents how good you were, instead of how bad!

In a speech delivered by Dr. Arthur F. Corey, State Executive Secretary of the California Teachers' Association, mention was made of a teacher who made the practice of writing what she termed, "The Letter of the Week."

According to the story, as the author recalls it, this teacher waited until she could observe some seemingly unimportant act such as picking up a piece of paper and dropping it into the wastebasket. Then, she sent to work! She tried to see to it that the Billy Bullies of her classroom were among the first to receive their letters.

One day she gave such a child a letter to take home to his mother. On the following day when the child arrived in his classroom, the teacher asked, "Did you give your letter to your mother?"

The child nodded.

"What did she say?" the teacher asked.

"Nothin'," he replied.

"Nothing? Why, it was a lovely letter—and your mother said *nothing?*"

The child nodded again. "She didn't say nothin'. She just bawled."

13 The Perennial Offender

When a teacher begins to establish conformity relative to adherence to accepted room standards for conduct, he will find the challenge an uphill climb. Initially one begins with an enlightened approach and treats all deviations from the expected norm lightly or as a temporary lapse of memory. The did-you-forget routine is effective to a point but can quickly lose its effectiveness, particularly when the same person or persons are forgetting a little too consistently and within shorter periods of time.

The offender then becomes chronic. In other words, he demonstrates that time is neither improving his memory nor his commitment to the room standards, toward which he made his contribution and toward which he voted his acceptance.

The offender, as well as the offense, in due time bring about their own *limiting factors* relative to *how much more* of the *same negative attitude and behavior* will be *tolerated.*

A teacher might say, "John, I have been most understanding in the past. I readily agree that it is sometimes difficult to remember our classroom standards, particularly when you become distracted or interested in something you are doing. But, John, I am growing increasingly concerned because you are making it so difficult for the rest of us who are trying to remember and make our classroom a good place in which to study. I must warn you that, if I have to remind you one more time, you will have to stay after school to make up the time you have lost by talking."

When John "forgets" and misbehaves again, the teacher approaches him and says, "John, I shall see you tonight after school."

Now, suppose that some five or ten minutes lapses and John displays the same kind of misbehavior again? What then? The wad has been shot and the pocket is empty. John is already coming in after school, now *what is left?*

One way of handling this situation is quite simple and quite effective. John is invited up to the teacher's desk for a clinical tête-à-tête. "John," the teacher begins, "you know that you are already staying after school tonight?"

John nods.

"Have you any idea how long you will be remaining after school tonight?"

John shakes his head.

"I'll tell you, John. I had intended to keep you fifteen minutes. That was when I spoke to you the first time. But, since you have once again disregarded my warning and have done the same thing a second time, you will now be staying twice as long."

John finds his tongue. "You mean I have to stay for THIRTY minutes?"

The teacher nods.

"Can't I stay for fifteen minutes? I won't do it again."

The teacher shakes his head.

So effective is this practice that eventually a teacher need not even speak to John other than to say, "tonight" and "double time."

It is most important, of course, that these after-school "appointments" be doled out with a smile. "It is nothing personal, you understand," the smile can say. "But, John dear, you and I are going to lick this thing if it takes us through the spring thaw."

Now, when a teacher detains a child after school, he had better make certain that the experience will be a memorable one. Too often, when a child is alone with his teacher in the classroom, the punitive experience develops into a dialogue of pleasant small talk. What punishment is this, when a child can chin himself on a teacher's desk and discuss with his teacher the relative merits of owning a pair of roller skates? These after-school experiences cannot even degenerate into a job-oriented approach such as cleaning the boards or stacking books. No indeed, this would be much too lovely.

"This is punishment?" a child might ask himself. "I'll do it *again* on the morrow."

An experienced teacher who has "been around the block" in terms of after-school hours, will tell of his routine with a dispassionate and clinical air. "It's a business arrangement. The child who wastes time or misbehaves in my classroom, has TIME to make up. It is as simple as that."

Some teachers begin the routine in the following manner. "John, now that everyone has gone home, you will have a nice quiet room in which to work. Would you kindly get a piece of paper?"

John ambles over to the table, picks up a piece of paper and returns to his desk.

"Now, John, I want you to think over this day. I want you to think about our room standards and I want you to think about your responsibilities as a classroom citizen. When you have finished thinking about why you are staying after school tonight, I want you to then write a composition which will tell me how you have assessed your behavior and how you intend to change it."

"Suppose I can't finish it in time?"

"In thirty minutes?"

John nods.

"I'm sure you can finish it, if your work very hard in this nice quiet room."

In some school districts there is a policy regulating the number of minutes a child may stay after school. Under these circumstances, an unfinished assignment can be completed at home.

It is the *unusual* child who does not respond to this consistent type of after-school treatment—particularly when the baseball season is on or when there are important after-school activities to attend. The nonchalance of the first after-school session quickly disappears when it becomes apparent to the offender that "it just isn't fun" to stay after school in the sterile atmosphere of a quiet room and close supervision.

If the teacher merely *threatens* to keep a child after school and then does nothing in terms of follow-through, the child will force his hand. If, in addition, a teacher keeps a child only momentarily after school with the warning, "I will excuse you tonight John, but tomorrow, if it happens again, I will certainly keep you for a longer period of time!"—then, the cause is surely lost!

John not only *knows* that the teacher is anxious to get home, but he carries this knowledge further by spreading the word that "after school" doesn't amount to a hill of beans. "She doesn't *mean* it," he tells his classmates.

The saving factor, in this situation, is that children *do not know* how desperately a teacher wants to leave when the teaching day is done. A teacher must trade on this by saying now and again, "I have all the time in the world, John. I don't mind staying after school. In fact, I rather enjoy it. I have so much time to get other things done."

However a teacher sets up his limitations on continual acts of disobedience, he should *follow through*. Whether it be the "after-school" routine, or asking the child to make up his work in his extra or free time, *some method for accepting the consequences* should be established and understood as a natural follow-through for deviant behavior. Otherwise, as in cases of civil disobedience, where laws are broken and the consequences for breaking the laws are neither offered nor accepted, negative behavior will be perpetuated, and respect for the law will never be achieved. In the classroom, behavioral standards represent the *law* in a child's social world.

Adherence to classroom behavioral standards not only helps in providing a favorable classroom climate for study but, in addition, creates a readiness toward respect and follow-through in the acceptance of social laws which govern the society of which the child is a member.

One may chose to liken classroom standards and/or social laws to red stop lights at busy intersections and/or to protective railings on either side of a high bridge. Cold logic will point up the fact that these limitations are protective, not impeding.

The perennial offender, indeed all children, need the security of *knowing that limitations exist* and the teacher's task will ever remain to provide the opportunities and experiences for learning them.

14 Efficacious Bouncing

There will be those times in a teacher's career where a child, for no apparent reason, will feel just feisty enough to attempt a showdown. Under these circumstances, it would be most imprudent to give in to one's natural impulses and attempt to "fight it out" with the child in the classroom. The odds would be against the teacher and definitely in favor of the child, in terms of a visual victory.

For example, let us suppose that a child's adrenal glands were working overtime, and, without warning or premeditation, he stood up and created quite a ruckus in the classroom.

His teacher rose to the occasion by standing up at full stature to counter with a comment that angered the child until his face grew red and then drained white. "Try and stop me!" he shouted back.

At this point the students gasped and watched their teacher assume a proper look of indignation, shock, and wrath. "Come here, this instant!" said the teacher.

But, lo! The child did not move. Instead, he put his hands on his hips and leered back at the teacher.

"Come here, I say!" shouted the teacher.

The child continued to stand his ground.

The teacher moved toward the child. At the same instant, the child moved backward. The teacher came closer, and the child moved farther back. Finally the teacher lunged at the child, whereupon the child pivoted around and ran to the front of the room into a neutral area. Now, the teacher's face grew red and then drained white. The children stared in disbelief. Again the teacher moved toward the child, and again the child ran into another neutral area. Eventually the teacher was chasing the child around the room. Somewhere on the second lap, the teacher heard the children laughing. It *was* a ludicrous situation. The child was always some twenty feet ahead. The child would *never* be caught by the teacher.

If anyone *was* caught, it was the teacher who snapped at the child's bait. The teacher lost. No one was happier because the situation developed into such a donnybrook. The child wasn't happier. He wished it had never happened. The teacher wasn't happier. He wished it had never happened. The students weren't happier. They did not really want to see their teacher appear so ridiculous.

At times of showdowns, it is always wiser to handle the situation with quiet and determined and decisive action. In this instance, the teacher should have walked to the child, taken him firmly by the hand, and walked out the door. Nothing needed to be said. Psychologists would call this action, "therapeutic bouncing." It *is* a form of therapy to remove a child from a happenstance that is beyond his ability to either understand or handle.

Once outside in the hall, on a one-to-one basis and away from the rest of the students, the teacher may look at the child and say, "I do not understand why you acted that way in class. I want you to understand that the behavior you exhibited in the classroom today, will never be tolerated. I am sure you understand why."

It is never wise to ask the child to "explain" himself or his actions, for he is too emotionally involved to think clearly.

Also, nine times out of ten, by the time the child is outside in the hall with his teacher, he will break down in tears. There is something therapeutic and healing about helping him to wipe his tears away with a damp paper towel and allowing him to get a drink of water. Afterwards, he will doubtless have himself fairly well in hand. The teacher may say to him at this time, "I would like to talk to you about this after school." The child is amenable at this point and is willing to yield under the temperant and rather mild consequences. He had really expected a good deal worse.

At this point, the door is swung open wide. All students look toward the door. They note that their errant classmate has been crying. The child enters ahead of the teacher and walks to his desk. The teacher has a cross look on his face. For all practical purposes, it appears as though the teacher has had the final and victorious "last word." Why not? The child was crying, wasn't he? The teacher looked cross, didn't he? The boy came into the classroom, much pacified, didn't he? No doubt about it. He got his just desserts!

The aforementioned narration explicitly stated that the teacher *followed* the child into the classroom. This is important. In this area of efficacious bouncing, more than one child who has followed a teacher has found the opportunity to "save face" by *making a face* at the teacher behind his back. Measure all probabilities and plug all openings! *Follow* the child inside.

Other types of "bouncings" take the form of making a child "sit it out" either in the hallway or in the principal's office. These are both rather foolish.

In the first place, the hall bouncing is too obvious. If and when a teacher practices this technique, it is usually run into the ground. More than one teacher has earned the reputation for being the school's "hall bouncer." Invariably, within the same school, the same teacher will have the same child sitting out in the hall. It becomes rather ludicrous after a time. "Can't that teacher handle that child in any other way?" The other teachers might ask.

Then, of course, the same can apply to the teacher who consistently applies the technique of sending a child to the office. He is the "office bouncer" who screams at children, "Go see the principal!"

Unless one has served in an administrator's role, it would be difficult to offer empathy. How weary the principal grows of seeing the same teacher bounce the same child into the office again and again and again! "Can't that teacher handle that child in any other way?" the principal might ask.

Beyond the tedium and the ludicrousness of such consistent practices in "hall bouncing" and "office bouncing" comes a more portentous cause for perusal. How do children react to the teacher who demonstrates consistently that he is second-in-command? How do children react to the teacher who demonstrates consistently that he is "defeated" by a certain child? How do the "bounced children" feel about their "bouncing"?

As in all things which are demonstrated over and over again in terms of reinforcing one's inability to handle control problems by alternate and varied means, the chronic "hall bouncer" and the chronic "office bouncer" quickly earn the reputation among students, colleagues, and administrator of being rather weak, rather devoid of resourcefulness, and rather Victorian. Later these evaluations are extended into the queries of, "Wonder if that teacher really *likes* teaching? Wonder if that teacher really *likes* children? Wonder if that teacher is feeling well? Wonder if that teacher is having some problems of his own?"

Be mindful that there is a difference between the efficacy of therapeutic bouncing, as opposed to the inefficacy of consistent and tedious "hall bouncing" and "office bouncing."

If the act of bouncing does not appear to treat or cure the child, then why perpetuate the practice of *only reacting angrily* to the *symptom* of misbehavior and of doing nothing to either *understand* or *change* the *cause?*

15 The Golden Rule Remains Golden

Although one would like to believe that progress has been made from the days of the hornbook, the dunce cap, and the hickory stick, some current practices among teachers continue to remind us that we are, as Emerson said, ". . . only at the cock crowing and the morning star."

Negative behavior on the part of students can often be a form of retaliation for the thoughtless words and deeds of teachers.

An adult recalls, "I was never a discipline problem until I reached the fifth grade. My teacher sent me to the office for something she accused me of doing, and yet I knew with a certainty that I had not done it. Thereafter, every word and action from her, elicited from me the wrong response. I took a sense of pride in being associated with her 'out group!' "

Adults have sharp recollections of their schoolday experiences, particularly if they were the recipient of sarcasm or humiliation. They remember the child who wore a dunce cap on his head, and they wondered in their enlightened years of maturity, "Was he retarded?"

They remember too, the time their teacher made them take everything out of their pockets because he did not believe them when they said they had not taken a child's dime.

When college students in education programs are asked if they remember a humiliating experience in their school experiences, they recall the day, the hour, and the moment.

"It destroyed my self-respect," one student said. "I was always on the shy side. A teacher accused me of laughing when she came into the classroom, so I was isolated in a single desk in the front of the room. I stayed there for the rest of the semester."

"I was frightened of my teacher," a student wrote. "She was a big person. When she would stomp up to me with that cross look on her face, I would start to cry even before she opened her mouth. She called me a 'cry baby' in front of my classmates. Everyone laughed. They called me a 'cry baby' for months afterwards."

It is often difficult for a teacher to assess himself objectively in his role. How does he appear to others? Particularly, how does he appear to his students?

In terms of size alone, let us examine a teacher as he appears to a small primary child. If the teacher is six feet tall, he is twice as tall as a child in the first grade, for example. Let us put this to a test. Picture, if you will, an adult standing before us who is twice as tall as we are. How tall would he be? Ten feet, eight inches tall? Twelve feet, four inches tall?

How would we react to this "giant" particularly if this giant looked angry or made threatening gestures or raised his voice in a resounding boom. Would we shudder? Would we quake?

Suppose that this giant moved jerkily around the room, heading in our direction, banging doors shut as he approached us, banging his fist upon desk tops and stomping his big feet. Would we feel threatened?

Suppose this giant made loud boiler-factory noises with his big mouth. Would we recoil?

How *different* this giant would appear if he stayed back in the peripheral areas and walked slowly as he approached us. How much *smaller* this giant would appear if, instead of standing tall and looking down on us, he took a little chair and sat down alongside of us, and looked at us on an eye level. How much more *gentle* this giant would appear if he would contain his large voice into a soft and gentle purr. And, how *friendly, approachable,* and *less awesome* this giant would appear if he consistently demonstrated by his actions that he was kind and fair and just. Finally, how *lovely* this giant would appear if he would *smile!*

We speak often of the Golden Rule and the efficacy of doing unto others as we would have others do unto us. But, do teachers really *understand* what these words mean in terms of their teaching role? Do teachers remember that they are working with children who are childlike, and not with adults who are adultlike? How often has a teacher said, "Act like an adult!"

"What is so wrong with childhood?" a parent asked. "I never knew until I was an adult that childhood was something to be cherished."

How often has a child been made to suffer humiliation for a childlike act?

Is a teacher devoid of sensitivity, or was it because he got up on the wrong side of his bed that he called that child "hopelessly stupid" in front of his classmates? Pity!

How about that teacher who makes a child sit in a corner, in front of his peers, with a dunce cap on his head? Never done in this day and age? Of course it is! With frightening regularity! But, how would *that* teacher feel, if his administrator told him to sit in a corner and gave him a dunce cap to put on his head—right there in a teachers' meeting, in front of his colleagues! Is *this* the test of the Golden Rule?

Did a teacher intercept a child's note which was sent to a friend? Did that teacher never write a note to his colleague during a meeting? A gentle warning is sufficient for the first time. Try not to make a big Federal Case out of a childlike act!

What *do* teachers *do* for those children who continually suffer the humiliation of reading in the same low-level reading group? Are they insensitive to the childrens' feelings and strive only to maintain the status quo? Do they apply the Golden Rule?

One teacher attacked the problem this way. "I allowed my slow learners to recreate a new image for themselves and others by allowing them to join the top reading group on a regular basis, every day. It should by understood that this practice was not to the exclusion of meeting in their own reading group with their easier material. Their own group reading lessons went on as scheduled, but, in addition, they were allowed to taste the delicious experience of holding in their hands a fat book with small print. Now, *I* knew that they could not read the material. *They* knew it. The other "smarter kids" doubtlessly knew it too. But, after all, what did it matter when ego was involved? At first, those little 'slow learners' made no attempt to try to read the words. Later, they were challenged. Finally, they were picking up familiar words and sentences. When this happened, I always called on them. They not only began to *read* like different children, they began to *look* like different children as well. It was a small inspiration of mine—to allow them to sit with the 'smart kids' and to hold in their hands, the books that 'the smart kids' always read."

A teacher may need the patience of a Job, but he does not

need the wisdom of a Solomon to ask, "How would I feel? Would my ego be quashed? Would my self-respect be shattered? Would I, perhaps, give vent to my feelings of frustration and attempt to retaliate?"

16 The Teacher Is Not a Peer Group

Miss X was young and pretty. She had a good scholastic record and a fine set of student teaching recommendations which proclaimed her strength in the area of creativity. She was hired by a school district as an eighth grade teacher.

To celebrate the signing of her teaching contract, Miss X went to Florida to do a bit of skin diving. She came home one day before school was to begin. But, my she looked *grand!* Her skin was tanned to an umber tone and her blonde hair, which had been bleached almost white by the sun and sea, hung softly to her shoulders.

When she entered school on the first day, it became apparent to her that the other teachers had been in their classrooms for almost a week in order to make preparations for the new school year.

"I don't believe in that sort of thing," she told a young teacher whom she had singled out as one who would be sympathetic. "This business about teacher-made room environments went out with high-button shoes! I intend to play it by ear and to allow my students to create their own environment according to their needs and interests."

When Miss X's students came into their room on that first day of school, they stood for a moment and looked around at the empty room. There wasn't even one picture tacked onto the wall. It was quite empty. Was this *their* room? Were they supposed to meet in *this* room? Had they made a mistake?

"Why don't we ask the principal?" someone asked.

"Ask him what?" a woman's voice countered.

The students turned and saw Miss X framed beautifully in the doorway. "Are *you* our new teacher?" they asked.

"That's right," she said. "Why don't you all sit down?"

There were a few low whistles from the eighth grade boys, while the girls said, "Isn't she *beautiful!*"

Somewhat in the stance of a skin diver as he stands on the edge of his boat contemplating his next dive, Miss X stood with her hands on her hips as she faced the class. She chatted with them for quite some time, interjecting here and there a large word, which would bring forth gasps from her students. "I have a teen-age brother," she said at last. "I believe I understand you quite well." She winked when she said that. The students giggled appreciatively.

In the last fifteen minutes of that first hour, Miss X explored the area of teen-age slang, and proved to them beyond the shadow of a doubt, that she was quite adept at following their jargon. She talked about their music and their dances. It was a heady experience for the students. Moreover, it was unbelievable. Too good to be true!

When the ten o'clock recess bell rang, the students were excused to go out on the playground. "Have we ever got a swingin' teacher!" they said. "She's a livin' doll!"

Miss X went to the teachers' lounge, lit a cigarette and blew a long stream of white smoke into the air. When a teacher asked how she liked her students, she said, "They're darlings! Every one of them, darlings!"

On those first days of school when the other students were becoming involved in a rather traditional approach to curriculum, Miss X allowed her students to watch the World Series on television. She had a perfect rationale for this. It took no major effort on her part to convince a somewhat skeptical principal that she was correlating physical education with arithmetic. "Children of this age group have a vital interest in the World Series," she explained. "I see no point in denying them this meaningful experience—particularly when *research says* that nothing is lost in a week's time. I believe that was Tinkerton's study," she concluded.

In the days that followed Miss X had taught her children how to make official looking score cards on the duplicating machine in the teachers' lounge. Albeit the duplicating machine, as well as the teachers' lounge, was reserved only for teachers, Miss X chose to pretend that she did not quite understand this directive. When she was admonished, she took it graciously, apologizing profusely.

In the classroom, she encouraged her students not only to keep score, but to cheer for their favorite team. When students began to "boo," she accepted this in her mind as part of the American mores. When her students disputed an umpire's decision, she called it "an exhibition of critical thinking." When they moaned audibly when a player missed a ball, she smiled. "It relieves hostilities and tensions," she said.

Finally the World Series was over, and Miss X took her students into the more structured area of solid curriculum. It was not her intent to make her students conform to the dictates of a curriculum pattern, but rather to make the curriculum conform to the dictates of her students' needs and interests.

Now, Miss X had some excellent colored underwater slides from her recent skin-diving expedition in Florida, and in her mind, under the circumstances, it would appear logical to use the slides as the needed stimuli in order to study geography with an oceanography emphasis. First, however, it would be necessary to motivate the children to the extent where they would say, as in one voice, "Miss X, let's study oceanography and relate it to geography!"

Yes, this was an excellent idea. "Children," she said. Then again, "Children."

The students were not listening to her. They were shouting and running about and acting for all the world as if they were sitting in the bleachers of a ball park.

"I have something to say to you. It is a surprise. Children. Children! Your teacher is talking to you!"

In spite of the colored slides on oceanography, as the days passed, her entreaties became more numerous and decidedly less controlled. "Keep quiet, I said. I am talking to you!"

Eventually, she employed the tactic of slamming her book down on her desk. "Now come on, kids, bring it down to a roar! What's wrong with you anyway? You're so rude. You're acting like first graders!"

At long last, she forgot herself entirely one morning, and, within earshot of the principal and the office secretary, she screeched, "Shut up, I say. Shut up!"

Somewhere in midsemester, at approximately ten o'clock in the morning, Miss X picked up her purse and stalked out of the room. She walked to her yellow convertible, revved up the motor, and drove away. No one was ever to see Miss X again.

When the eighth graders were told that their teacher would not be returning, they said nothing. In fact it could be said that they took it rather stoically.

A girl in the back of the room said softly to her friend, "I don't really care. I was getting sort of tired of hearing her scream all day long, weren't you?"

The substitute teacher who replaced Miss X was again, a very young and very pretty teacher.

"I assume you have a course of study you wish me to follow?" she said to the principal when he hired her.

"Yes," he said with a distinct feeling of relief, "I'll get you a copy."

In short order, the very pretty substitute had the eighth grade students productively engaged in matters pertaining to tried-and-tested eighth grade curriculum. There was no lead-up other than for her to say, "We have a job ahead of us if we are going to cover all of this material by the end of the semester. Remember, you are going to have to prepare yourselves to enter high school."

When the principal came into the substitute's classroom to observe her teaching, she was not even aware that he had come in the door. Few students turned around to look at him sitting there in the back of the room. They were too busy.

"How did you do it?" the principal asked her, when the students had left the room. "Why, they don't look like the same unruly youngsters I observed in here a week ago."

"Unruly? Unruly! These children? Why, they're *darlings*. Every one of them, *darlings*," said the substitute!

17 But I Really Want to Be Loved!

Everyone wants to be loved. Everyone wants to be respected. Even the teacher, who would like to feel that his students think of him as being fair and square, brave and honest, intelligent and talented, and even funny. It would boost a teacher's ego tremendously if he knew, with a degree of certainty, that his students ran home each night, threw open the doors, and shouted out, "Do you know what? *My* teacher is the *best teacher* in the world!"

The sad facts of life persist in reminding us that students are not apt to do this, particularly when their teacher is committed to the area of establishing classroom control in those initial and crucial first weeks of school. If a child is pressed for an evaluation of his "new teacher," he is more apt to say, "I liked my other teacher better."

Verily, it is during these times, that a teacher stands alone and lonely, strong and strongest. These are his finest hours.

A master of classroom control and a most popular teacher said, "I suppose you might call me a friendly dictator. It takes me about six weeks of dogged plugging, without the reprieve of letup, before I have my classroom control where I want it to be. During that time, my students merely tolerate me. I'm sure that they picture me as a tough taskmaster. That's precisely the impression I set out to create. One of my students said, 'She has eyes in the back of her head. You can't get away with *anything* in *this* class! What a teacher!'

"Whenever I hear comments such as these, I don't allow them to upset me, although I must confess that in my earlier years of teaching they upset me a great deal. Now, I am more clinical in my lack of reaction. My students are not talking about me as I *am;* they are talking about me as I *appear.* Therefore, my hide has become as thick as a Hippo's. I remind myself that I am not in the teaching role to win a popularity contest. This is basic to my thinking and my long-range goal. My aim is to be an effective teacher in a wholesome classroom climate. While my students are assessing me, wondering whether or not they are going to like me, I have already made up my mind that I am going to like them just fine. Therein lies the difference. I keep projecting to the weeks ahead, when we can all relax and have fun, *within the limitations of established standards for classroom behavior.*"

This teacher was saying, in effect, that *a tightly held reign can be loosened at a projected date, but a loosely held reign can seldom be tightened.*

It is rather easy for an experienced teacher to feel the security of knowing that eventually he is going to be loved and respected. What of the new teacher? The inexperienced teacher? The neophyte? The ineffectual teacher? What assurances lie for them?

The answer to this is simple. The same assurances lie for them that were guaranteed to the experienced teacher when he was new, inexperienced, ineffectual, and/or a neophyte in the profession. The beginning swimmer swims hardest when his feet cannot touch the bottom of the pool. He may be frightened and he may be alone, but the challenge calls forth resourcefulness and brings to bear all that he ever knew about moving and keeping his head above water. When he makes it to the other side, deep water will never again appear as dangerous and as awesome as it did when he looked at it from the baby pool. Perhaps his stroke was indefinable, perhaps he remembered it not at all, but it did the job; it was functional. In the days that lie ahead, he can think less about sinking and more about technique. For now, he can be satisfied that he did not sink; he swam.

The American writer, Christian Nestell Bovee said, "A failure establishes only this, that our determination to succeed was not strong enough."

George Elliot, English novelist said, "Character is not cut in marble; it is not something solid and unalterable. It is something living and changing. . . ."

One of the incongruities of the teaching profession lies in the truism that those teachers who aim to please and seek to be loved, are seldom those teachers whom children ultimately like and respect. The teacher who tries to reach a child by coming down to his level, by becoming one of his peer group in allowing himself to be addressed by his first or last name only, is on his way to oblivion. Children prefer that their teachers exhibit an adult attitude with a wholesome reserve of dignity.

Insensitivities lie with all manner of teacher-behavior, not only with attitudes. For example, the teacher who wears a red form-fitting knit dress, when a less obvious attire would elicit fewer comments from her children, is indeed flirting with negative factors relating to control and respect. The same applies to a lesser degree to the teacher who wears dramatic and sweeping earrings, sophisticated hairdos, and charm bracelets that jingle jangle jingle.

Other factors which bear thoughtful analysis are: the predeliction to laugh out loud and lose control when it would be more prudent for the moment to muffle the guffaw and maintain the control; the leaning toward using slang when it would be more befitting in one's role to use proper English and sustain the tone of the teacher-model; the weakening effect of exhibiting bad manners when one has been insisting that "everyone should be polite"; and generally tolerating disorder after much time has been expended in articulating expectations for order in classroom behavior.

Who are the teachers that children never forget? Which teachers do *you* remember? Do you remember the spineless ones who always allowed you to get away with your classroom behavioral shennanigans? Do you remember the sticky-sweet ones who did nothing more than smile and smile some more? Hardly.

The teachers that children remember and never forget are those teachers who showed them very early in the game that the classroom was to be respected as a learning laboratory and that *there were limitations* for social behavior. These teachers were firm but, in addition, they were fair and square, brave and honest, intelligent and talented, and even funny. In short, they were, to their children, everything a teacher hopes he will be—a smashing success! These teachers who are remembered were not only consistent in maintenance of their standards but were persistent in seeing that the classroom remained in a favorable climate for study, work, and growth. And last, but certainly not least, these teachers whom children remember *taught them something!* Whether it was to wash their hands before lunch, to excuse themselves when they were rude, to manipulate numbers in a systematic way, to find the beauty of the written or spoken word, or to be inordinately grateful for the opportunity to live in a democratic society—whatever it was, it was remembered and relished because it was taught in depth. Too often, teachers forget that children really want to learn and are happiest when they are confronted with the challenge of achieving.

Beyond this, these teachers were resourceful, decisive, sensitive, and warm, remembering always that they had a responsibility to maintain their adult role as a model for emulation. This was the kind of dignity that befitted their profession.

These were the teachers that children never forgot. These were the teachers that children never ceased loving. Long after they became adults and had children of their own, they became reflective and said often, "I'll always remember my fifth grade teacher—"

18 Trippingly on the Tongue

If the voice can be considered an instrument, the teacher, then, is the instrumentalist.

As beautiful music is the potential for all instruments, beautiful sounds are the potential for all teachers' voices.

We know, for example, that some of the sounds of music are brassy, harsh, and loud, as in a marching band at half time in a football stadium. Sometimes these sounds of music are angelic and soft as in the music boxes which would lull babies to sleep. And sometimes, the sounds are varied, now medium, now soft, now rising into a crescendo, as in a symphonic selection.

However these sounds of music come for the occasion, there is the qualitative factor of skill and interpretation that measure the music in terms of good, bad, better, and best. So let it be with the sounds that come from the instrument of the voice!

Which voices find most appeal? Those which always shout and screech, so that one feels compelled to clap one's hands over one's ears? Those which always remain in such a low range and pitch that one feels compelled to cup one's hand around one's better ear in horn fashion? Or, is it the voice which is at medium-low pitch and is neither excessively loud nor excessively soft? Is not the most appealing voice the latter?

Which category is most appealing within the range of the medium-low voice? One which is always excessively excited? One which is always clinical sounding and lackluster? Or, is it the voice which would rise slightly when excited, drop lowly when serious, and maintain a soothing equilibrium in expository narrative? Is not the most appealing category within the medium-low voice the latter? One which would direct us and motivate us and give us clues?

The French philosopher Voltaire said, "Use, do not abuse; abstinence nor excess never renders a man happy!" So let it be applied to the use and abuse, abstinence and excess of the voice instrument!

Vocal cords can be strained and students' ability to "hear," at the same time, can be impaired when a teacher is endowed with a healthy set of lungs and persists in his desire to use them often in order to achieve full volume.

In Chapter 5, "Contentment is a Pretty Room," it was stated that a teacher should greet his students on the first day of school with a soft voice that would barely penetrate the warp and weft of the delicate fabric of *beginning right*. As a teacher speaks, so goes his classroom! Speak loud, and the noise level will be established. Speak low and a vast range is left for future exploitation.

It is not unusual for a group of students to assume a noise level beyond all reasonable means simply because their teacher speaks consistently in a loud voice. Student might ask themselves, "Why be quiet? Our teacher always shouts above our noises."

On the other hand, the teacher who begins with a light touch, with a minimum of exertion of the vocal cords, quickly establishes the mean for noise levels within his classrooms. "I am speaking low," he might say to himself, "because I want my children to learn to work quietly. Only then, can they hear me."

If such a teacher ever needs his students' attention, a quick inflection or a simple rise in sound projection, will gain that attention, for it would be an *unusual sound*, not more of the same.

Teachers who use their voices at high range and pitch all the time find it difficult to gain their students' attention. Such teachers can shout at maximum volume and have nothing happen. Soon they are restoring to blowing whistles or clanging gongs. This is highly perilous. For again, a louder range of sound is established for response.

Veteran teachers in the profession utilize the voice trick of speaking low initially. When a situation occurs where control is threatened, instead of falling into the obvious trap of raising the voice, they purposely LOWER it. Children who may have allowed their attention to wander are awakened and brought back into the fold by this simple device of utilizing a new and softer sound. They will lean forward and will listen with more intensity. It is a simple trick, universally practiced, and proven for its effectiveness!

A second grade teacher, who was a master of control, consistently utilized the medium-low range and pitch of voice. One day she came to school with laryngitis. Under this extreme condition of voicelessness, she conducted her class with complete control by gestures and written directions on the board. Impossible? Not at all.

As in all things, it should be remembered that the sameness of anything becomes a crashing bore. A low voice consistently practiced, without inflection, can be deadly. The vast potential of the voice as an instrument would point up the fact that it can be varied to soothe and calm or to excite and motivate. It takes a degree of sensitivity to know when these times become propitious in terms of soothing and calming and of exciting and motivating. Pace the voice. Make it work for you as a teacher, in terms of both *effectiveness and economy*.

There is, of course, such a thing as *talking too much* and for *too long a period of time*. Some teachers do this because they have not planned well enough. They use vocabularies which are not atuned to the grade in which they are teaching. They are not *clear* with their directions. They repeat themselves, saying the same thing over and over again and again, thinking perhaps that if they perpetuate the muddle by extending their narration, it will all magically somehow appear clear. A simple checking point for these teachers is the query, "Are there any questions?"

Some teachers talk too much because they are nervous. They begin every sentence with the word "well" and/or they repeat out loud every response a child offers. Talking, for these teachers, is a substitute for biting their nails.

And finally, some teachers talk too much because they suspect (and rightly so) that no one is listening to them. They say, "If you do not pay attention, I will *not* repeat this a second time."

But of course they *will* repeat it, and they *do* repeat it, over and over, again and again.

If children do not listen when their teacher is talking to them, it is because they have been conditioned to believe that their teacher does *not expect them to listen*—at least, not for the first time. It is like the child who does not answer his mother's call until she calls him for the third time. He has been conditioned as effectively as one of Pavlov's dogs. The first and second calls mean nothing. His mother knows this as well as he does. So why answer?

It is the wise teacher who will *not speak* until *everyone* is listening. If it means that the teacher will be forced to stop what he is saying and wait, then by all means WAIT. If it means that the teacher will have to stop a second time, or a third time, then stop and WAIT. Silent teacher disapproval and exasperated peer disapproval is too strong a factor to override. Soon enough the offenders will understand that when *their* teacher talks, *everyone listens* because *their* teacher will not talk when someone is not listening. Moreover, *their* teacher *means it* when he says, "I will not repeat this a second time."

There is nothing more to it than that. If a teacher allows himself to overlook rudeness, he will receive rudeness in return. Children will respond either to the *highest* or to the *lowest* of teacher-expectations.

In terms of voice economy, a teacher must also become sensitized to the sound of his own voice. "Have I been talking too much this hour? I have? Very well then, it is time I shut myself off."

If a teacher does not check himself in this area, he will not have the opportunity to shut himself off. His students will do it for him. Students will grow so accustomed to *that voice* which drones on and on that they will eventually become neutralized to the sound of it.

If a teacher would like to test his voice effectiveness and/or lack of it, a tape recorder provides one of the most meaningful and revealing evaluations. Turn it on when the school day begins, and then play it back after the children have gone home. Chances are one will find himself saying, "Oh dear. Oh dear. Oh dear!"

There are many ways of saving the voice both in terms of vocal cord preservation and in terms of control. Suppose a teacher spots a control problem in the far corner of the room? Should he shout across the room in order to quell it, thereby disturbing and distracting others? Certainly not! Walk to the corner of the room and whisper in the ears of the offenders. Often times, it is not even necessary to whisper. Simply standing next to the offenders, making one's physical presence known, is enough to regain control.

The voice can also be saved by employing some of the accepted attention-attracting devices. Some teachers tap their desk tops with the side of a half-dollar coin, others tap a small desk bell, others strike chords on the piano, and still others flick the lights on and off.

If the voice is used in an effective and economic manner, teachers will seldom offer the common complaint, "My voice is *so* tired! I am going home tonight, and I am not going to talk to anyone!"

Prithee, thou rememberest the somewhat indelicate phrase, "the whiskey voice"? Verily, it is sometimes more applicable to the shouting and tea-drinking teacher than it is to the silent and potted sot!

19 Veni, Vidi, Vici!

Common in the early practices of the inexperienced and ineffectual teachers is their persistence in employing their range of vision to their lessons plans and to the board but rarely to their students and/or to the long-range type of observations which are so necessary in the perceptive analysis of *what is really going on* in the classroom. In spite of their prominent position at front and center, some teachers become so unwholesomely engrossed in their subject matter, and the sequential development of the same, that they can be likened to the city slicker who attempted to bring the cows home to the barn without looking behind to see if they were following. Students, like the cows, can return to the pasture, leaving the teacher alone when he reaches the barn door.

When a teacher attempts to present a lesson to his students, he must always employ a range of vision which is at once, both direct and sweeping, focused and peripheral, looking directly at that child whose span is short and then again at the group as a whole.

In Chapter 18, "Trippingly on the Tongue," mention was made of using the voice effectively. It was stated that no teacher should attempt to address his class until all children were listening. It was also stated that teachers should avoid disrupting other working children by shouting reprimands and directives across the room.

There is still another method of stopping negative behavior while a teacher is talking and presenting a lesson. This method mentions the child's name within the context of one's oratory, not in an angry manner, but in a clinical almost dispassionate tone of voice. Either in affirmation of fact, or in query, a teacher might begin, "The California Indians were well known for their excellence in basket weaving. I believe, CHARLES, that the basket you wove last week will give you some appreciation of the kind of skill that is involved in basketry. The California Indians were also peace loving. Were they not, SALLY?"

In the longer passages, and in recapitulation of narration, the same tool may be applied, never stopping to point up an infraction when children begin to drowse or stray from acceptable standards for behavior but, rather, continuing to intersperse the offender's names: "We all know that the California Indians lived along the coastal area long before the Spanish Explorers arrived. You reported yesterday, JOHN, that the Indians were most resourceful. JOHN said yesterday that the Indians lived off the land. Is that right, TOM? Yes, TOM, you remember. I am sure that both SALLY and BETTY will remember how interesting it was to learn that the Yosemite Valley was a chief source of food for the Indians. Why was that, PETRANELLA? Very good. They hunted there, didn't they? Where did they get their salt, CHARLES? Of course, from the salt beds near the ocean. Wasn't it interesting to find out how they collected their salt? Do you suppose, PETRANELLA, that if we put sticks into salt beds that we could collect salt on them? Should we try that some day?"

If and when a teacher finds it necessary to go to the blackboard in order to make notations relative to facts gleaned from research, he will most effectively meet the needs and demands of control by involving the students in the context of what is going to be written. He would also benefit by placing himself at an oblique angle to the board rather than facing it in a parallel manner. The oblique angle allows the teacher to look around as he writes—at once keeping his eyes on his students and the blackboard. The parallel placement would bring about complete closure with the teacher's back facing the children. Most dangerous!

Keeping the children gainfully employed, through involvement, is likewise of portentous significance in all matters relating to control.

"How shall we write this?" a teacher might ask his students. "Will you spell 'California Indians' for me as I write it on the board, CHARLES? Let us all listen carefully as CHARLES spells 'California Indians.' Let us see if he can do it without making a mistake. This is not very easy CHARLES, but try, will you?"

Teachers can modify and extend these simplified methods of maintaining control during discussion and blackboard-writing periods, to suit temperament and individual needs. The most basic factor to remember is that *vision* should work as intensely as methodology. Neither can be separated. Both work hand in hand.

In the Book of Proverbs, it is stated, "Where there is no vision, the people perish."

See, not only in the focused and peripheral manner, but, *see* and remember. Why is John so sleepy? Why is Sally's attention span so short? Why does Charles turn his head and cup his hand over his ear when something is said to him? Do their expressions indicate that our discussions are being understood, related, and assimilated?

See, and fact-find.

See, and evaluate.

See, and grow as a teacher.

Develop the sensitivity to sharpen one's skill to *see* purposefully.

20 On Hoisting the White Flag

In Chapter 10, "On Giving In for the Moment," it was stated that a teacher should develop a perceptual awareness in terms of not adhering to unrealistic goals and expectations, *for the moment*. The metaphor was created which pictured *gains* as being swept out into the ocean in a frightful undertow. The teacher was advised to keep his head above water and to swim with the tide until he could manipulate the unfavorable situation into more positive action.

A distinction, therefore, exists between those areas in the establishment of classroom control, which *can* be teacher manipulated and those which *cannot*.

Inasmuch as this book has articulated for the most part those areas which are manipulative, this chapter alone will offer a statement on the imponderables, or those areas which can rarely be teacher manipulated toward positive results.

At certain predictable and unpredictable times in one's teaching career, there will appear those days which will remain unalterable in their totally absolute, utter, and complete chaos. Despite elaborate planning, positive attitudes, knowledgeableness, good mental health, and proper rest and diet, *everything* will go wrong.

On these days it would be supportive, as an ego-sustaining device, to walk casually into the teachers' lounge and, in an equally casual manner, ask a teaching colleague, "How were your children, today?"

The teacher to whom the query was addressed might give

the questioner a studied look and then might say, "Rather stimulated. And, yours?"

"Higher than an intercontinental ballistic missile on a successful launch."

From across the room a teacher will look up from the rim of a coffee cup and will say, "Yours too? Mine are impossible!"

What are these factors of commonality, comprehensiveness, and all-inclusiveness, which outfox teacher preparedness, experience, and skill? Why do these times of little response, excessive activity, and retrogression occur? The reasons are many and diversified; a partial listing is as follows:

1. Times preceding and following school assemblies, movies, plays, etc.

2. The class picture-taking day.

3. Visitors in the classroom during Public Schools Week, etc.

4. Days of medical examinations, eye examinations, hearing tests, speech tests, inoculations, shots, and polio sugar cubes, etc.

5. The advent of holidays such as Halloween, Valentine's Day, etc.

6. Period preceding spring vacation.

7. Period preceding the closing of school and/or promotions and graduations.

8. The advent of parties within the classroom or the advent of parties outside the classroom.

9. Construction within earshot and eyeshot of the classroom.

10. Repairmen or maintenance men within the classroom, such as plumbers, electricians, window washers, etc.

11. Disruptions which alter routine, such as a stalled school

bus, late hot-lunch program, loose dog on the playground, bees in the classroom, ants in the lunch boxes, etc.

12. Mechanical failures, such as a short in the bell system, a heating failure, plumbing failure, electrical failure, etc.

13. Rain, sleet, snow, wind, hail, earthquakes, fires, etc.

14. Fire drills, air-raid drills, etc.

Aside from these easily pictured experiences, there are other more indefinable and less visual occurrences which disrupt control. For example, this author believes that barometric pressure can work positively or negatively in the maintenance of classroom control. It has been reported that when barometric pressure drops under conditions of extreme cold waves, the body chemistry will change. During those periods which precede a rainstorm, which would not necessarily bring about a cold wave, body chemistry will change also.

It is a well-known fact that those who suffer from high blood pressure will experience a marked increase in systolic pressure in periods of extreme cold. It is a fact that blood pressure rises during barometric change in periods of extreme cold and in periods preceding a storm, and, in addition, the adrenal glands are rendered more active.

Some interesting subjects for doctoral dissertations are opened to teachers who wish to explore the influence of barometric rise and fall on body chemistry and subsequent classroom behavior.

These imponderables relate to those mysteriously ideal days as well when, in spite of a teacher's lack of planning, his negative attitudes, his lack of knowledgeableness, his poor mental health, and his inadequate rest and diet, and under the most bland of teaching stimuli, sudents will perform with the optimum reasonableness, attentiveness, and cooperation.

The score is evened, however, when it becomes apparent to the thoughtful teacher that at either extreme (on these smashingly good and on the horrendously bad days) one's effectiveness in matters of control cannot be measured with any degree of validity.

It is *those* times and *those* days that lie in between which divide the men from the boys, the successful from the unsuccessful, and the effectual from the ineffectual. These are the times of needed knowledgeableness, manipulation, and skill. Sadly, luck has little to do with it.

The best a teacher can do when these unalterable absolutes appear is to hold himself steady and say with conviction, "This, too, shall pass."

It always does.

21 It's Clean-Up Time!

Upon retirement, a supervisor of general curriculum said, "At last! I will never again have to witness another clean-up period!"

An art supervisor said, concurrent with his daily observations, "It is enough to give me ulcers. Whenever a teacher looks at the clock and appears unduly distressed, I know what's coming next! He will shout, 'It's CLEAN UP TIME!' I want to run for cover—and usually do."

A young classroom teacher said, "As soon as I say, 'It's clean-up time,' the sky falls down!"

Without borrowing undue pessimism, it can be stated that clean-up time can be, and often is, a horrendous experience. The problem, however difficult, *can* be conquered.

In a hypothetical illustration of a finger-painting experience for an entire class, it will become apparent that, from its inception to its conclusion, *P&O is evident.*

Before the lesson begins, children are covered with smocks, desks are covered with newspapers, drying areas for wet paintings are covered with newspapers, supplies and materials are available in needed quantities and are ready for distribution.

Should the children begin, now?

Not yet.

The children are called to the front of the room where chairs are available for seating and a table is prepared for the teacher's demonstration. Motivation begins in terms of the possibilities and limitations of the finger paint as the teacher demonstrates the technique and articulates the process in a step-by-step progression. She is finished.

Should the children be dismissed to go to their seats and begin?

Not Yet.

Certain monitorships are needed in terms of supplies and their distribution. What are these monitorships and who shall these monitors be? The teacher lists both on the board.

Now, are the children ready to begin?

Not yet.

"We will need some clean-up monitors at 9:40 when our painting period will end."

What are these monitorships and who shall these monitors be? Again, the teacher lists both on the board.

Now, *surely*, the children are ready to begin?

Not yet.

"We will need a sink monitor, someone who will assume the responsibility of seeing that not more than two children are at the sink to wash their hands." Another child is chosen. "Now remember children," the teacher says, "you will have to receive permission from Bobby before you will be able to wash your hands at clean-up time. I think it would be a good idea, Bobby, if you only chose those children who had put their smocks away and were seated at their desks."

Are the children ready to begin, *yet*?

Not yet.

"Do you understand how to pick up your wet paintings?" the teacher asks. "Do you understand where your wet paintings are to be placed when you are finished?"

The children nod.

Certainly, *everything* is in readiness?

Not yet.

A general discussion follows relating to the expectations for clean-up.

Now, ARE THEY READY?

Not yet.

"Are there any questions?" the teacher asks.

"Can we paint two pictures?" a child asks.

"If you think you can finish both of them before 9:40 and do a good job with both."

"What if you aren't finished at 9:40?" a child asks.

"You will have to judge your own time. That is *your* responsibility," the teacher says.

"What do we do when we're finished?" another child queries.

"Can anyone answer Jimmy's question?" the teacher asks.

"Look at the Extra-Time Chart," a child answers.

"Certainly. You may make up your unfinished work, read a library book, any number of things."

Now, are they ready to begin?

Yes, they are ready to begin. Preplanning is done, motivation and demonstration are done, child planning is done, expectations are articulated, questions are answered; yes, they are ready to begin painting.

The clean-up period does not always relate to an art experience, but sometimes rather to another experience, such as "group research," where diversified materials are also used. In such instances, children within those specific groups may cooperatively assume responsibilities for clean-up.

A teacher who worked with primary youngsters used to ask her children to seat themselves on chairs in a semicircle when they had finished their clean-up after social studies. Her purpose in doing this was to assemble the children for their evaluation. It goes without saying that, in this type of arrangement, some children would be seated long before others. What of them and the possibilities for losing control as they sat in their chairs, unsupervised, with nothing to do? This was the answer! The teacher planned it so that there would be a degree of pride attached to their early arrival at the semicircle of chairs. As soon as the first five children arrived, they would write their names on the board and state the time of their arrival. It may be stated with a certainty, that there was no glory attendant on an early arriver, if his clean-up responsibility was not efficiently done!

Beyond this, the teacher employed another trick. Children were instructed to take their seats according to the time of their arrival. The earliest arriver sat at the end, while the second-earliest arriver sat second from the end, and so on. The first child then, would begin singing a song of his choice with the other seated children singing with him. When the song was finished, it was understood that the second arriver would have his opportunity to begin singing a song of *his* choice, and so on, until all the children were seated in the semicircle. When the teacher finished the last-minute observations of their clean up and attended to necessary related details and finally made her way to the semicircle to join the students, EVERYONE WOULD BE GAINFULLY EMPLOYED, SINGING HAPPILY with no control problems either in sight or on the horizon.

Try it!

A final bit of advice comes from a supervisor who said, "Beginning teachers usually make the error of not allowing themselves *enough time* for clean-up periods. As a rule of thumb, I tell my student teachers to *double* the time they think is adequate. Gradually, it can be trimmed down. It is always better to end up *with time to spare,* rather than with not enough."

22 That Smashingly Quiet Hour

The teacher who grows in his ability to develop the complete utilization of his perceptual senses, will eventually be able to see, hear, feel, taste, and smell the tenor of his group. On a particular hour or a particular day, if the perceptual senses indicate that it is a time for caution, then improvization and adaptation can be brought into play in terms of seeking effective alternatives to planned curriculum.

For example, let us suppose that on a particular morning, a teacher sensed that his students were unduly agitated, distracted, uncooperative, and/or unwholesomely loud and vociferous. His lesson plans indicated that in ten short minutes, he would provide for them a finger-painting experience. What would he do about it? Would he rush pell-mell into disaster by following his lesson plans to the letter? Or, would he find the guidance and the wisdom to provide a less catastrophe-prone art experience such as the crayon etching or crayon sgraffito processes?

It is entirely within the realm of reason that a flexible teacher might find himself phasing out the art experience entirely and using instead an alternate calming device, such as reading aloud a chapter from a book.

Under the circumstances of agitation, distraction, uncooperativeness, and/or loud vociferousness, *any and all alterna-*

tives would be preferable to the finger-painting experience which by its very nature demands the highest kind of order in conduct.

As a teacher grows in his role, he not only becomes more knowledgeable and more perceptive, but becomes more practical. He accumulates what, for lack of a better name, may be called "a bag of tricks." These are exactly what the name implies, an interesting and awe-inspiring collection of proficiencies which calm, sooth, and beguile. While the "bag of tricks" could not be called profound and would miss its mark in terms of related and correlated curriculum, it nevertheless serves a purpose in terms of reestablishing classroom control. In addition, this bag of tricks may be called, somewhat facetiously, *teacher-status boosters.*

For example, the teacher who masters some clever paper folding and cutting techniques (as in paper sculpture) or some equally clever three-dimensional folding techniques (as in Japanese Origami) will find himself with some excellent *calming* tools. The anticipatory surprise element is there. Something is going to happen, but *what?*

"Sit down now, and watch the way I fold my paper. Do you know what this is going to be? No? Very well then, wait. Now, look at the way I am cutting over these folds."

"What's it going to be?" a child asks.

"A surprise. Look very carefully now, or you will miss it."

Quiet. More quiet. Serene. More serene. "Ah," says the teacher, "*for the first time today, I have them in the palm of my hand. Careful now. Work slowly. Don't lose it. Keep the voice down. Whisper. Whisper. Whisper.*"

"What's it going to be?" the same child *whispers.*

"Wait now. I will open it. Look. An expandable bird cage!"

"Aw, that's neat. Can you do another one?"

"All right. I won't tell you what I am going to do. Look carefully and see if you can guess."

And, so it goes. Total and complete mesmerization. With what? Just a few tricks pulled out of an emergency bag—all usefully designed and collected by the teacher to shut little mouths and to glue little seats to chairs where they sit.

What others are there? Is the teacher an amateur magician? Wonderful! Is the teacher proficient with science experiments? Grand. Does the teacher collect poetry? Good. Does the teacher play an instrument? Very good. Does the teacher have a good collection of phonograph records? Fine—particularly Brahms (not Stravinsky)! How about taking the children outside for a few running laps around the playfield? This is effective. Whether inductively induced or deductively deduced, the quiet hour can come, and will come, to that teacher who practices *resourcefulness*.

Following lesson plans meticulously, when all indications point up the fact that it would be in error, *is not the mark of the good teacher*. When students are neither ready nor responsive to *the best laid plans*, control often goes astray. And, in the final analysis, what is *really* achieved under negative circumstances. Do they really learn? Do they remember? Do they relate and assimilate?

If teachers feel a sense of guilt in bypassing what is supposed to be taught at a particular hour, let them practice the art of *pretending*. Pretend that you *did* follow your plans. And pretend that nothing was gained, nothing was retained. Pretend again, that the same lesson had to be taught all over again on the following day (as indeed it often is). And when it is presented on the following day, under more favorable circumstances, pretend that it is coming to them for the second time. What has *really* been lost?

23 When Nothing Works

Life has its peaks as well as its valleys and, with the numerical element of chance being what it is, one can be assured that somewhere along one's professional progression toward seniority there will appear that time when a teacher will fall heir to a group of students who will have earned the reputation of being "the worst class in the school."

At these traumatic times, teachers often forget how many good classes preceded them and, also, how favorable the chances are that good classes will follow. For the nonce, under the pressures of reality, where the past is forgotten and the future is dimmed by the terminable aspect of "the formidable class," teachers have been known to say, *"If it wasn't for bad luck, I wouldn't have any luck at all!"*

It is as difficult to apply rules of logic to the *whys* and *wherefores* of problem classes, as it is to apply rules of logic to the approximate ratio of one to seven. Perhaps it can be explained in the Oriental belief that one is accorded in his lifetime a cycle of seven years of good luck and then seven years of bad. However one explains it, the prognosis is not hopeless.

Certainly when these problem classes arrive, a teacher's *skill* and *resourcefulness* are tested, as well as his *endurance*. One without the other could be likened to an egg without salt. One is sustenance, the other makes sustenance palatable.

A primary teacher once found herself in a coveted new position in a demonstration school. As luck would have it, in that first year of trial when her ability in her role was being assessed, she fell heir to a classroom full of second graders who were termed by one and all, as being "a most difficult class."

She struggled nobly for awhile, steadfastly applying all known devices toward the establishment of classroom control. As the days and weeks wore on, she was forced to admit that her thirty youngsters were no nearer being *under control* than they were on the first day of school.

"Nothing works," she said to herself as she drove home one evening, "nothing at all."

This admission was a difficult one for her. She had never known failure as a classroom teacher. Indeed, it was *because* of her ten-year record of teaching success, that she was sought and hired as a demonstration teacher. Now, she was admitting to herself that she was somewhat overrated and that she was not really up to the task. She drove aimlessly that afternoon. She thought of failure and how she would accept it when it came with the knowledge that she would not be rehired for the coming year. What would she do? Go back to her former school district and say, "It didn't work out."

The longer she drove, the deeper were her thought processes. With the deepening of her thinking, the more she knew she could not accept failure. She would *have to succeed.* But how?

The next thing she knew, she had parked her car and had entered a toy shop. She examined all of the imported and domestic toys, games, puzzles, and books. Finally she had made a selection.

"You must have many children," the clerk said to her as he tallied her items and rang the total on the register.

"I do," she said, "thirty."

"Teacher?"

She nodded.

"Doesn't your school provide some of these things?" the clerk asked.

"Some," she said. "Not all."

"You're spending a lot of money here," the clerk said as he handed her several large packages.

She got to school very early the next morning and set all of the colorful, shiny, new, and intriguing toys, games, puzzles, and books, on a table in the front of the classroom. Then, she cut some tagboard into small rectangles. On these she lettered the words GOOD CITIZEN.

When the children arrived that morning and saw the wonderful things on the front table, they started opening them, examining them, and commenting on them. Eventually this gave way to snatching, pulling, tugging, and cries of indignation. "I saw it first," one said.

"No you didn't. It's mine! It's mine!"

The teacher walked to the table and rearranged all of the toys, games, puzzles, and books as they had been before. "These don't belong to anyone," she said. "Not just yet. Why don't you all sit down and we will talk about to whom these things really belong."

Every child scampered to his seat and sat down.

"Is everyone listening?" the teacher asked.

"BE QUIET!" one of the children shouted. "The teacher wants to tell us something."

"That's right. Everyone will have to be quiet in order to hear me when I explain how you will be able to use these wonderful new things that you have seen on this front table. Can you do that? Can you be quiet while I explain?"

The heads nodded.

"Let us look at some of these things more carefully," the teacher said. Then, one by one, every game, toy, puzzle and book was held up and shown to the children.

"Oh boy, those are neat!"

"Shhhhhhhh!" a child cautioned, "we're supposed to be quiet."

"Very good," said the teacher. "I am glad you remembered."

"*When* can we use them?" a child shouted from across the room.

"When you are *good citizens*," the teacher said.

"WHAT's a good citizenthhhhh?" the children chorused.

"Does anyone know what a good citizen is?" the teacher asked.

"Someone who doesn't talk?"

"It's much more than that. A good citizen talks only when it is necessary, and he knows *how to listen* when the teacher is talking. He doesn't talk to his neighbor when he is supposed to be working at his desk. He raises his hand when he wants to say something important, instead of shouting across the room at the teacher. A good citizen is courteous, and he is kind."

The room became exceedingly quiet.

"A good citizen," the teacher continued, "is able to sit next to his neighbor at lunchtime without fighting, pushing, or shoving. He is able to use good table manners in the cafeteria, even when the teacher is not there. He keeps his voice down and is generally able to work and play well."

"I do all those things," a chief offender shouted.

"Ah, but you see, you have already done something that a good citizen would *never* do. You talked without raising your hand."

Immediately the child raised his hand.

"Yes, Dennis?"

"I do *all of those things*," Dennis said once again.

"I am glad to hear that, Dennis. You should be a good citizen very shortly." The teacher then picked up the packet of cards with the elaborate lettering which said on the face of each, GOOD CITIZEN. "These cards will be given to you when you have become a good citizen. When you have one of these cards and when you have finished all of your work, you may bring your card to this lovely table, leave it here, and take a toy, game, puzzle or book of your choice. When you have finished, you may return it, and take back your card."

"Can you do it again, tomorrow?"

"Oh yes, once you earn a good citizen's card, it is *yours* to keep, UNLESS you forget yourself and I am forced to take it away from you. Then, you will have to earn it all over again. It would be much better, when you have earned it, to plan on keeping it for all time, wouldn't it?"

A child forgot himself and shouted, "Sure!"

"Boy, you're sure never going to be a good citizen," another child said.

"Neither will you," another child said, "you talked without raising your hand!"

"So did you, smarty!"

In the second hour the teacher looked directly at a child and said, "I have been watching you Mary. You seem to be working very well, and you seem to be remembering our room standards. I believe you are ready for one of these cards. Children, *Mary is our first good citizen.*"

When Mary was finished with her assignment, she took her card to the table and selected the most choice game. She took it to her seat and began to open the box and take out one piece after another.

Every child in that classroom stopped what he was doing and looked at Mary with envious eyes. Mary rattled the pieces and smiled and purred. It was all quite lovely. The children became more industrious, more quiet, and more determined than ever to become *good citizens* with all of the rights and privileges thereunto appertaining.

That was how control began, and that was how chaos ended because eventually, *everyone* was a good citizen. By that time, the toys, games, puzzles, and books, looked less new and more worn. But the feat had been accomplished. The children became productive with their new-found work habits and found the kind of unique satisfaction that comes from learning. Classroom control was achieved. The teacher then was able to demonstrate her real ability which was commensurate with her experience and skill. She knew all along that she was never *that bad* as a teacher. But, she had to prove it to herself before she could prove it to her students, their parents, and others.

Some purists in education might argue that this teacher arrived at her goal through the back door. "She offered a reward," they might scoff. "She should have tried to reach the children through alternate channels—speaking to them and appealing to their reason."

Not so. She had tried that. She had literally exhausted every means at her disposal. *The teacher does neither himself nor his students a favor by perpetuating the climate of failure.*

She had said, had she not, "Nothing works!"

She weighed the evidence both in terms of the children's lack of social and academic progress and in terms of the pressures which realistically existed for her—specifically, to demonstrate her effectiveness in her new role. Time was of the essence.

If one believes that this teacher *did indeed* employ somewhat primitive and archaic means in dealing with the problem at hand, she did it because time and circumstance demanded drastic action. She met the children on their own ground and spoke to them in the terms they could understand. Reward, and/or bribery if you will, were the efficacious means for response *at that time*.

To have sought to continue the practice of speaking to them when no one was listening, to have sought to appeal, one more time, to their reason when there was no base for expecting sound judgment, that would have been a massive blunder!

A basic teaching premise says that *we must take children where they are and bring them as far as we can* in a given semester.

If children are woefully immature and unskilled, we identify that lack of maturity and lack of skillfulness and then take it from there, hopefully onward and upward.

We cannot teach a pollywog how to jump simply because he gives promise of one day becoming a frog. Nor can we assiduously cut off his tail in order to hasten his development.

When the games and the puzzles and the toys had lost their lustre, so had deviant behavior. In its stead were good work habits and the joy that comes when spewed energies are harnessed into the productive and meaningful tasks attendant on learning.

In the end, the children forgot about striving to become good citizens because they just were good citizens. They understood that when their work was finished they could still go to the table and select anything they wished. It was a transition toward growth and for them, a satisfying one.

The teacher did well.

24 A Parent-ing We Will Go!

It had been "just one of those days" for Miss Pinkerton. If anyone had asked her about it, she would have said, "I just couldn't get a handle on it."

It had begun in the before-school hours when one of her second grade boys had gotten his zipper stuck. By the time she had taken him back into the classroom, someone had overturned the goldfish bowl. She had a mop in her hands when the principal walked through the door and said, "May I present our new board members, Miss Pinkerton? They would like to visit in your classroom this morning."

At approximately three o'clock in the afternoon, Miss Pinkerton's head had begun to throb. By 3:29, the throbbing had developed into an awesome, full-blown migraine.

She reached into her desk drawer to take out a bottle of aspirin tablets and at that precise moment, the teacher next door came into her room to remind her that if she did not hurry she would be late for the Hospitality Hour in the auditorium.

The first parent gathering of the new semester was scheduled to begin at 3:30—a fact that had totally escaped Miss Pinkerton. She put the bottle of aspirin tablets into her purse, for there would be no time to take them now.

"I will just have to make the best of it," she sighed. "My, but I do wish that I could go home and lie down."

Most of the mothers had already arrived when Miss Pinkerton made her entrance into the auditorium. The mothers looked freshly showered and chic; garnished with sprigs of daphne and scented with perfume.

Unbeknown to Miss Pinkerton, her dress bore, in the back, a purple jagged chalk mark. Her stockings sagged a bit at the knees, and her hair appeared as if she had held it under a rotary beater at a medium speed setting.

"There's one of our teachers," a mother chirped.

"Oh yes, Miss Pinkerton," said a second mother.

"Miss Pinkerton?" the third mother said. "Why, she is Bobby's teacher! I must run over and tell her that *I* am Bobby's mother."

The woman ran over to Miss Pinkerton and grabbed her by the elbow. "Miss Pinkerton! Miss Pinkerton! *I* am Bobby's mother!"

"Isn't that nice," said Miss Pinkerton as she nodded and continued to make her way toward an empty seat in the first row. *Who is Bobby?* she asked herself as she sat down between two flowered and furred mothers.

Miss Pinkerton picked up the scent of Chanel on her right and of nicotine on her left. She plopped two aspirin tablets into her mouth as soon as the entertainment chairman stood up to make her opening statement.

"We have a surprise for you today," the entertainment chairman began. "The local drama group in our community has requested me to remind you that their annual subscription drive has begun. One of their members, Mrs. Thespian, is here with us today to perform in one of her own original readings. You may recall that last Fall, during the World Series, she performed in a reading called, 'Casey at the Bat.' "

Miss Pinkerton nodded. She remembered.

"We all know of Mrs. Thespian's long and illustrious career in drama circuits in the upper midwest. I am sure that she is largely responsible for bringing. . . ." The entertainment chairman looked furtively down at her notes and then continued, ". . . for bringing a quality of excellence to our community theater. And now, without further ado, may I present Mrs. Thespian, who will interpret her own and original composition, 'Climbing Life's Ladder!' "

The mothers and teachers applauded generously as Mrs. Thespian arose and stood before them, bowing ever so gently now to the right a bit, now to the left, and now at dead center.

Miss Pinkerton sighed heavily and began to chew her aspirins vigorously.

Mrs. Thespian took her position before the group, folded her hands in front of her, closed her eyes, and opened her mouth to begin when a child's voice was heard emanating from the back of the auditorium. This was followed by a mother's voice emanating from the back of the auditorium. There was some scuffling and, then, pattering of feet as both child and mother tip-toed out the rear door.

All the while Mrs. Thespian stood motionless before the group with her hands folded and her eyes closed. Eventually, all was still and Mrs. Thespian began in earnest. With a dramatic thrust of her voice (which very nearly shot the tender head of Miss Pinkerton off its unstable pinnings), Mrs. Thespian shouted, "I have climbed life's ladder!"

Miss Pinkerton shifted her position in her chair, furrowed her brow, and instinctively touched her temples with her fingertips.

"I have climbed life's ladder," Mrs. Thespian continued, "and this say (pause), this I say (pause), this I say (pause) again! I say this again (pause), again (pause), and again (longer pause).

All right, Thespie, Miss Pinkerton sighed, *let's have it. What DO you say?*

"... I say *this* to you again, and again, and again! Be wary, be wary, be wary!"

Oh dear, Miss Pinkerton thought, *this is going to be worse than I expected.*

"Be wary (pause), be wary (pause), BE WARY . . . OF THE FORMLESS MAN!"

Well now, THAT'S worth hearing! I run into formless men quite often in my profession. Miss Pinkerton cleared her throat hard.

"Do you have a cold, dear?" the Chanel mother asked.

"A slight one," Miss Pinkerton said. "I have been trying to fight it off."

The Chanel mother gave Miss Pinkerton a look of compassion while the nicotine mother leaned over to whisper, "Would you mind if I had a cigarette?"

"... The formless man is coming! He is coming (pause), coming (pause), COMING! He is coming for all of us (pause) ... who fear!"

That's me, Miss Pinkerton thought. *I fear. I fear I am not going to be able to take much more of this. Well, all right now, here comes the formless man! Now, where are we on life's ladder, Thespie? Are we still on that wretched first rung? I feel weak. I almost feel like laughing. She's looking at me. I'll nod and smile at her. Now, what did you do THAT for? You didn't have to smile that broadly! Be careful!*

"... I fear you, oh formless man! I fear (pause), I fear (pause), I fear (much longer pause)."

Thespie doesn't look like she would have to fear anyone. Wonder what size she is? 44?

". . . Do not fear me, little one. Do not fear. Fear not, little one!"

"Snnnnnffffftttttchcctttmmmmmpfff!" *How did THAT come out of me? Good grief! I had better try to patch it up with a few coughs.* "Cough, cough, cough." *Yes, that was fine. It even sounded wheezy. Be careful now. You are weaker than you imagine!*

". . . I will take you to a world of TRAWNQUILITEE, and of LAHfter. I will take you to a place where the sun ne'er sets!"

Please don't let me laugh out loud again, here in front of everyone, Miss Pinkerton asked with her eyes cast toward the ceiling. Look at me. I'm helpless. I'm tired. EVERYONE is here. The principal, the teachers, the parents. I mean, she has only BEGUN to climb that ladder! We have been sitting here for—ONLY five minutes?

Wonder what would happen if I took five aspirins? Would I pass out? Suppose I didn't?

Mrs. Thespian had leaned down to pat out a rhythm on the piano stool. "Pat-a-tat-tat. Patt-a-tattt-tattt!"

Let me think of all of the sad things that have happened to me. Yes, that was terribly sad. Then, why am I smiling? That was really SAD. That's better. And then, there was that time when you introduced Jim Tribley to your cousin Gloria, THAT was sad! Remember when you broke your leg on the ski slope? No one was around. Remember how long you lay there? Wasn't that sad?

". . . Hear those beating drums? Come with me to where life throbs and awaits thee and me. Come. We will skip through the daffodils into the sunshine that lies ahead."

"SNNNNNFFFFFfftttttcccch . . . fft . . . ft!" *I did it again!*

This is ridiculous. I am making a fool of myself. Imagine laughing like a teen-ager! I am a TEACHER! "Cough, cough." *I am a teacher who does not have tenure or permanency!* "Cough, cough, cough." *If only I could leave. But how? Where's the door? Why did I ever sit up here in front? I'll cough a little bit more, that may help.* "Cough, cough." *That's better. Now, cross your legs. Pull your dress down over your sagging stockings. Bite your lip hard if you have to. How hard can you bite your lip without having it bleed? Am I bleeding? I wonder if I am bleeding? I shall take out my mirror and see. Good grief! I had no idea that I was smiling that much!*

". . . skipping, skipping, skipping. 'You and I,' said the formless man."

I've got to get out of here fast. "Snnnfffftttt!" *Put your handkerchief over your mouth! Cough, hard! No, you fool! You're going to laugh again.* "Smffttt!" *You see! You did it again! Honestly! You are standing up in front of everyone now. This is your last chance. DIGNIFY your exit! Cough again. There! Harder, now.* "COUGH, COUGH, COUGH! Snnn-nnffffftttt!" *Get out! Get out, fast. Better run. There's the door. Gangway! All right, you made it. Now, cough up a storm out here so that everyone can hear you inside. HARDER! HARDER!*

"For goodness sake," a voice said. "Miss Pinkerton. Miss Pinkerton. Are you all right?"

Miss Pinkerton looked up. It was Bobby's mother. "Yes, I am all right. It is really nothing."

"But, are you quite sure, my dear?"

"Quite sure. I have been living with this for quite some time," said Miss Pinkerton.

"Do you think a drink of water might help?"

"Yes, I think that would help."

"Let me get it for you—"

"Oh no, Bobby's mother—ha, ha! No, no, I mean. I can get it."

"But, it's no bother to me. I would be happy to do it!"

"I wouldn't want to deprive you of the opportunity of hearing Mrs. Thespian," Miss Pinkerton said. "I mean, she is SO GOOD. I just wouldn't want you to miss her performance because of me."

"I don't mind, dear. I have heard it before. Mind you, it is QUITE GOOD!"

"Oh my, yes!"

"Let's go get that drink of water," said Bobby's mother. "I believe I could use some myself."

Pity, thought Miss Pinkerton, *she is such a decent sort, and, with all of that, I STILL CANNOT REMEMBER BOBBY!*

NOTE: This bit of satire, offered in the realm of comic-relief, does not mean in any way to detract from the multifarious good works of parent-teacher organizations, clubs, and associations. In the area of classroom control, communication is necessary and these groups are to be respected for having promoted cooperative working relationships between parent, teacher, and child. Had Miss Pinkerton not been suffering from a migraine, and had the events of the teaching day been less horrendous, she might have remembered Bobby as the boy who overturned the goldfish bowl!

25 It's Tuesday Already!

While a high degree of knowledgeableness is important in one's professional role, so is a high degree of commitment and positive attitude. Without the latter, one's existence is dull, flat, and untenable. A misalliance between a teacher and his chosen field can bring its own unique kind of dissatisfaction, and that dissatisfaction can bring its own unique kind of ineffectiveness in matters relating to control.

In Chapter 1, "When Common Sense Appears Uncommon," it was stated that it will never be enough for a teacher to say, "I know how I am here." Rather, it needs be, "I know *why!*" For, unlike other professions where clientele must be courted and won through a continual demonstration of skill in the building of a reputation for excellence of performance in the competitive market, the teaching profession is literally *guaranteed* a booming business! In dealing with the multitudes, it might be well for the teacher to remind himself, from time to time, that his "clients" are there because of compulsory laws relating to attendance. The task, therefore, in demonstrating skill and excellence of performance, with an optimum of purposefulness, would relate directly to one's own personal concept of integrity within the framework of professional ethics.

Firm commitment and positive dedication, in terms of supplying the needed answers to the query, "Why I am here?" can never be found by attempting to enter the profession through the back door—with "in-spite-of" rationale. Rather, it is the primacy of the "because of" factors which would supply their own valid entry toward sure direction and ensuing satisfaction. An attempt to compromise on this premise would bring about a calamitous invalidation of professional choice and would result in a totality of disservice for all concerned.

In lacking felt commitment and dedication toward the day by day promulgation of the teaching task, and in lacking sincere motivation toward achieving a quality of excellence in the performance of one's role, a teacher might be likened to an inept aerialist who is literally "holding on by his teeth." In lurching from crisis to crisis with an attitude that could best be described as one of neurotic stability, such a teacher is unwholesomely prone toward the building-up of fears, frustrations, and anxieties. In giving what he considers to be *more,* he continually receives what he considers to be *less.* His is the demonstration of the law of diminishing returns.

When emotional satisfactions are lacking, both in the act of giving and in the act of receiving, the teacher stands on precarious ground, for all people need to feel that they have accomplished something, whether these accomplishments be major or minor.

Unfortunately, negative attitudes and lack of enthusiasms can never be quelled by attempting to hide them, no more than in attempting to hide them can they be quelled. They transmit themselves, in their deadliness, from teacher to student, from student to parent, from parent to principal, and, finally, from principal to teacher.

A student may say, "I don't like school any more."

A parent may say, "Think I will call the principal and ask if Johnny can be transferred into that *nice* teacher's classroom."

A principal may sigh and say, "That's the second call this

week. Wonder what's *wrong* with that teacher? Think I had better do a little observing in her classroom this afternoon and then have a talk with her."

The teacher is defensive. "I'm quite tired. What I really need is a vacation."

While it is true that a weekend in the snow or a summer on the beach can do much to recharge worn down batteries, it would be sheer folly to build one's continual rationale on these terms alone. The days, weeks, and months that lie in between will continue to be both taxing and demanding, and the teacher will continue to need the additive of remunerative regeneration which comes only when reciprocity of satisfaction occurs.

Every profession has its misfits. Teaching is no exception. There are those who have persisted in remaining in the class-room despite the fact that they accrue nothing in terms of either giving or receiving. But on the other side of the coin, there have been those teachers who have faced the facts squarely and have made the decision to leave. In having found more satisfying endeavors in alternate choices for livelihood, they have neither returned to the profession nor entertained any regrets for having left the fold. Still others, who have left the profession to seek out their alternatives, found that, in time, they *did* have regrets, and *have* returned, usually far better teachers for having made the change.

A teacher expressed it this way, "I felt as if the walls were coming in at me. I wanted to try my hand at something else. I took a year's leave and became a saleswoman in an import gift shop. It was a good experience, but after awhile, when the newness wore off, I had time to assess what I had given up. I am not sorry that I gave up teaching for awhile and then returned to it a year later. I don't believe that I could have ever appreciated my profession so thoroughly unless I had that time for assimilation and that experience for comparison. The teaching job is unique in its long-range satisfactions. Sometimes you have to walk away in order to know why you must remain. I know I did."

An administrator added, "A happy teacher is a good teacher. Whenever a teacher confronts me with his dissatisfactions in his role, I tell him to remove the cause. Nothing is more important in my school than maintaining a teacher's good mental health because, when it's poor, it affects everyone—students, administrators, parents, custodians, special services personnel, secretaries, and even other teachers. I encourage teachers to accept better teaching offers, and I encourage them to return to the Islands to teach—if that's where they would rather be. I can always find substitute teachers for the interim periods. Believe me," he said, "I would much rather have a smiling substitute than a permanent teacher who scowls."

Parenthetically, it should be stated that *many* people train for special professional roles and then eventually find themselves working in a totally different field. This is not unusual. There is no social stigma attached to one who has the wisdom to admit that he has made a miscalculation in terms of his professional bent and direction. Such people are to be congratulated for having made the effort to find their satisfactions in a world that is made up of many alternatives in terms of choices. This is not to say that attitudes cannot be changed. It would be most disheartening if the teaching field lost potentially good and strong professionals simply because there was an acceptance of negativism as an inalterable way of life.

A successful curriculum consultant recalls her early years

in teaching when she was unsure of herself in terms of having made the right decision in entering the profession.

"I was quite young and immature," she recalled. "I was wholly dissatisfied with my position as a fourth grade teacher because I fancied somehow that I belonged in a more exciting milieu. I had gotten on the bus one afternoon to meet a friend of mine in the city. Quite by chance, I saw a former college classmate in the bus and sat down next to her.

" 'What are you doing now?' she asked me.

" 'Teaching.'

" 'Really? I'm a teacher too,' she said. 'Isn't it wonderful?'

"I gave her a long glance and then I said, 'No, I can't truthfully say that it is *wonderful*. The fact is, I have been asking myself whether or not I made a mistake.'

" 'You?'

"I nodded. 'I don't know what it is—or what it isn't for that matter. Sometimes I wonder if I can hold on until summer comes.'

" 'That's a fine attitude in *January*, she said.

"I sighed. 'I know it.'

" 'What are you doing in your classroom?' she asked me.

" 'Oh, the usual. Reading, writing, arithmetic, spelling.'

" 'That's rather bare-boned, isn't it?'

"I nodded.

" 'Have you ever thought of giving it the old college try?'

" 'What do you mean ?'

" 'I mean, *make it more exciting!*'

" 'But, I don't feel like making it exciting. If what I am doing is drab, it is a reflection of how I feel.'

" 'How do you really *know* how you feel unless you see some return?'

" 'Like what?'

" 'Let me tell you something,' she said, 'The more you put into your teaching day, the more you will receive in return.'

"My friend did not say much thereafter about our respective teaching roles. I suppose she thought that I was quite hopeless. But what she didn't know was that I remembered what she had told me. I returned to my classroom the next day and said to myself, 'You have a good six months before summer comes. So, why *don't* you make it *more exciting?*'

"Thereafter, I noticed the change in the children's faces. They were looking at their *new teacher* in disbelief. She was smiling. She was arranging field trips for them. She was showing them movies. She was inviting guest lecturers into the classroom. She was even bringing them small candy treats that she thought they might enjoy.

"I had to remind myself from time to time that my smile was just 'pasted on' and that 'I really wasn't enjoying it.' The truth of the matter was that I had found the worth of my friend's statement. 'The more you put into your teaching day, the more you will receive in return.'

"Perhaps, for her, at the time, it was a platitude, but for me, at the time, it struck a responsive cord. It showed me that nothing worth doing comes easily, and one's satisfaction in any role is commensurate with investment.

"In the years that followed, when my success as a classroom teacher was assured and I went into administration, I was able to detect who those teachers were 'who were merely holding on.' I saw the same kind of lackluster expression that I once wore.

" 'Let me tell you something,' I would say to them, 'the more you put into your teaching day, the more you will receive in return. Put in nothing, and you get nothing. Put in everything, and it comes back a thousandfold.' "

26 Teacher Conservation Program

Perhaps no one area of professional endeavor is more demanding of sound emotional equilibrium than that of teaching. In receiving the joys and rewards attendant to the day-by-day promulgation of the teaching task, one falls heir, as well, to the day-by-day disappointments and frustrations. The latter accrue as natural by-products when one is dealing in numbers of students as well as the individual differences and needs within these numbers. Alas, it will ever be thus, for one hand washes the other.

In consistently attempting to meet the challenges head-on, one must pause from time to time if only to gain one's perspective. Perhaps this perspective will come by accepting the fact that even teachers are endowed with those factors pertaining to human limitations, in given circumstances and/or on given days. Perhaps this perspective will come with the knowledge that meaningful attainment of one's professional goals does not come without vast expenditures of effort. As the Chinese philosopher-artist Po-Chu said, "To express an idea or to represent an object properly, it must be turned over and over in the mind until it unites with the soul."

In seeking Po-Chu's particular kind of philosophical fusion in the teaching role, one would concur that any attempt to perform with a high degree of excellence in one's chosen discipline *is* most taxing and *can* drain one of his emotional reserves. Unfortunately in teaching, when one is committed to the consistent demonstration of sustained high gear operational facility, one does not call momentary recesses when the spirit moves him. The degree of effort needed in the classroom is not always equitably distributed on the calendar. When a teacher feels weakest, it is usually then that he must have strength; when a teacher feels strongest, it is usually then that he will need little of that strength!

In remembering that a teacher serves as a model for emulation, even during those times when he *thinks* he is not being observed, responses and attitudes, in terms of how one accepts disappointments and frustrations, become areas for perusal. Whether or not a teacher it actively engaged in teaching per se, he is usually always being observed by some student. In being observed, learning is taking place. Such learning can be catagorized as *incidental,* but it is no less effectively assimlated into the totality of educational processes.

Does a teacher demonstrate a low tolerance for mishaps and calamities when they occur?

Yes? *Pity!*

No? *Bravo!*

The teacher who, when the bell signals a fire-drill, is mixing a bucket of plaster of paris at the sink is faced with two alternatives. He may either give vent to an emotional outburst (which incidentally will do nothing to retard the hardening of the plaster) or he may more realistically rise to the occasion, take his children outside, and think more propitiously of where he is going to find a hammer when he returns to the classroom and faces the solid mass at the sink!

In assessing the need for equilibrium and positive responses, the teacher should, very early in his career, chart out his own individualized program directed toward maximum promulgation and conservation in the all important area of mental health.

The preceding chapter made a plea for finding one's sincere commitment and dedication to the profession. This is the first step. Secondly, there is a rather famous aphorism which, when committed to memory, will help to establish a healthy and sustaining point of view:

> God grant me the serenity to accept
> those things I cannot change,
> Courage to change the things I can,
> And wisdom to know the difference.

Disappointments and frustrations will never appear as being awesomely insurmountable when one learns to grow *purposefully* toward emotional and intellectual maturity. This statement would relate to the teacher in his role as a demonstrating-evaluator, as well as to the student in his role as an observing-learner. *The development of the whole child in the classroom learning milieu can only reach fruition when the development of the whole teacher is an actuality, not merely an illusion which is measured in terms of inches, pounds, and years.*

Beyond those areas of commitment, dedication, positiveness, and growth, what other areas need identification and exploitation? Quite obviously in the conservation of mental health, proper rest and diet are necessary. When these are lacks, responses become shaky. Planning and organizing helps, and so does the program of shared responsibilities among one's students. Knowing policies and procedures with unhalting assurance saves repetition of effort and needless retracking.

Promoting good working relationships among one's parents will likewise prove beneficial. Support of one's colleagues and administrators will negate involvement in cliques, gossip sessions, and/or school politics. Beyond this, outside the classroom, *a change of pace as well as a change of scene becomes a practical necessity!*

' Despite what armchair philosophers may say to the contrary, living outside the boundaries of one's school or district will help immeasurably to cast off the cares of the teaching day. Of course, if one is hopelessly committed to the philosophy of total integration, in associating continually with one's students and one's parents, and if one does not mind his role as chief disseminator of information relating to school holidays, reporting periods, opening and closing dates of school, and various other policies and procedures regarding school business, then, by all means, live within one's school boundaries, and be glad! It would be just as unfair to say that all teachers would respond negatively to living within one's school boundaries as it would be to say that all teachers would respond positively to such geographical home-site limitations. School districts in the past years have become more and more liberalized in terms of insisting that their teachers live within close proximity to their schools. This liberalization of policy is happily accepted by the majority who revere the concept of individual differences and/or preferences.

It is also important to develop a set of interests which may be totally divorced from one's teaching profession. Attendance at the theater, symphony, or opera is beneficial. Enrollment in evening classes which feature courses in ceramics, weaving, mosaics, and other craft activities will not only help to develop a new set of interests but, at the same time, will offer the therapeutic value which comes from release in involvement. Spectator sports are good, but participating sports are better!

A concerted effort to divorce oneself from educational jargon and traveling in circles with people from all walks of life is likewise of value. Teachers have often been ridiculed for their tendency toward inbreeding, ingrowth, and ingrouping. While they may function perfectly in a given social situation which is dominated by nonprofessionals, given the chance of an opening, by spying a fellow teacher in the crowd, the ball is tossed, received, and run with, leaving fellow companions alone and bewildered by the ensuing exchange of teacher talk. Learning to grow *in* one's profession is one thing, but learning to grow *out* from it is quite another. Both are important in the development of the whole teacher in his quest for mental health, for each part belongs to the whole and each part takes, as well as gives, as the teacher relates both to the inside and the outside of his classroom.

Someone made the observation that a teacher's day was never-ending. When the last school bell has rung, there are papers and workbooks to correct, plans to formulate, and forms to type out in triplicate. Manifold problem areas are left unsolved and these consume a teacher's consciousness with a persistence that is all-pervading.

A word of caution is appropriate to those inexperienced teachers who would stay in their classrooms hours after everyone else has left for home. While a degree of this can be expected in those first crucial months in the profession, the continual practice of keeping late hours should be discouraged. Enlightened administrators are sensitive to this problem area. While on one hand they may rejoice over a teacher's conscientiousness, on the other, they often worry about Miss Jones or

Mr. Smith who "always seems to be working here so late in the evenings." More than one administrator has counseled his overly conscientious teachers to "go home early tonight and get a fresh start tomorrow."

Inexperienced neophytes in the profession are often panic stricken at the prospect of leaving earlier. They watch the experienced teachers get into their cars and drive away. How can they do it and teach so well? When do they get all of their work done?

A closer examination of the situation would reveal that most inexperienced and "overly conscientious" teachers either waste time and/or consume time in needless little rituals which, in the end, neither improve nor impede their teaching performance. Such a teacher was once observed, at seven in the evening, dusting autumn leaves on the science table!

Now hear this: *The teacher who survives his teaching role and lives to teach another day is that teacher who can walk out of his classroom, after a reasonable number of hours, with no guilt feelings relating to that which remains to be done.* Such a teacher must adopt as his professional credo, "I have done what I can, and I have done what I must. Tomorrow will take care of some of it and, with a little bit of luck, time will take care of the rest."

In closing the door, both literally and figuratively, a teacher is able to, on one hand, shut off his teaching role and, on the other hand, assume his private and avocational interests. One role can never be totally divorced from the other, for each role, in turn, both gives and takes sustenance—alone and together and at the same time running. But, in the development of the whole teacher who would ultimately seek to aid in the development of the whole child, this spirit of reciprocity of growth, in both vocation and avocation, must realistically exist if self-directed teacher conservation programs are to succeed and prosper.

27 These Teachers I Try to Forget

"All cruelty springs from weakness"—Seneca.

I was afraid of my fourth grade teacher. She had a violent temper. More than on an occasional basis, she would punctuate her wrath by slamming a closet door or by throwing a book across the room.

Her temper rose to its peak at arithmetic time, for it disturbed her when students "missed" their arithmetic problems. When she would return our papers from the previous day's assignment, she would stop at each student's desk, in turn, and would berate them in her loud voice.

One day as she was reprimanding one of the boys in our classroom, she noted that he had turned pale.

"What's wrong with you?" she asked.

"I don't feel good," he said.

"Put your head down until you feel better," she instructed him. And then she walked away.

So deeply did this bit of drama impress me and become engrained in my consciousness that the very next day when the teacher approached me with my arithmetic paper, I said, "I don't feel good."

"What's wrong with you?" she asked.

"I've got a stomachache," I lied.

"Put your head down on your desk until you feel better."

For the rest of the arithmetic period, while the other students worked on their assignments for that day, I hid my head in my arms feigning illness. It pleased me that I would miss out on the next day's evaluation of my arithmetic work. So heady was my success, that I tried it again the next day. It worked again. However, on the third day when I once again tried it, my teacher excused me, but called my mother to report that I had a somewhat chronic problem which merited a doctor's attention.

After the doctor's examination, I had to take some tiny pills. My mother wrote a note to the teacher saying that the doctor suggested that, if and when I became ill in class again, I was to be allowed to rest.

For the rest of the semester, I became "ill" during the arithmetic lesson, and made my recovery as soon as it was over.

Hard to believe? Not at all. It happened precisely the way I have recorded it!

My fifth grade teacher was insensitive to the feelings of her students. That is why I did not like her. She took the path of least resistance, never pausing to consider alternate and less humiliating ways of choosing sides for kickball teams.

Every day, it seemed, the same group of children alternated as being team captains. Their likes and dislikes were always expressed in the same way. Pity the poor child who was always chosen last, as I was!

Often, a captain would say, "Do we have to have *him?*" . . . .

When that happened, I always waited for a miracle which would lift me up and out of the classroom. But, that miracle never happened. Not even my teacher reacted to what the captains would say. She was too busy with her thoughts while she was buffing her nails.

I never forgot the humiliation which was needlessly heaped upon me and others by lazy teachers. When our graded papers were passed back to us, teachers would call out our names so that we could call back our grades while she recorded them in her book. In my mind, this was an invasion of my privacy.

I had a sixth grade teacher who was crotchety and ill-tempered. I was never able to please her.

I knew that she liked wild flowers; hence I would spend many hours in the hills in back of our home, tracking down wild flowers for her science table display. One day she said, "The wild orchid is almost impossible to find!"

This was my challenge. I looked and looked until I found one blooming near a brook in a wooded area. The next day, I literally ran all the way to school.

"Look," I said. "I found a wild orchid!"

Her response was mild and most disappointing. She merely took the flower and put it into a mason jar and then labeled it as a wild orchid.

I was crestfallen. I knew I could never win her affection. After that experience, I knew that I could not even *buy* her affection. There was nothing left except to *endure* the long and painful semester.

My fourth grade teacher gave every child in the classroom a part in a puppet play, except me and another child who had a speech impediment.

When the puppet play was presented for the entire school in the auditorium, the doors were thrown open and everyone in my class marched down the aisles with a puppet in his hands —except me and the other child.

When our classmates marched onto the stage, we two children alone, stayed behind to sit in an empty section of chairs which was reserved for our class. It was humiliating and crushing for both of us.

I never understood why I was denied a part in that puppet production. It remained for a long time, one of the great mysteries of my childhood. I had memorized every part. I knew how to work the curtains and how to dim the lights. I was a cooperative child. Why?

In adulthood, I understood that it could have been as simple as—my teacher not liking me.

When I graduated from college as the valedictorian, it should have erased the memory of my fourth grade experience. But, I still remember it as one of the most searing experiences of my childhood. It was cruel and it was so unnecessary.

During the depression years, my ninth grade teacher was making a concerted effort to achieve a 100% banking record in our classroom.

In order to open a bank account, it was necessary to make an initial deposit of one dollar. As this amount represented approximately 5% of my father's weekly wage, I was never able to open an account.

I remember those long mornings when my teacher would stand before us and lecture to us on the efficacy of saving money. Gradually the number of bank accounts increased.

Finally, there were but two of us who remained without bank books. Again the teacher lectured to us and told us how desperately she wanted to win the 100% Banking Banner.

The next day there was another account opened, and I alone remained as the abstainer. Again, the lectures came.

I shall never forget how my mother dug down into her purse to bring up a dollar bill which had been folded several times. "Let's go to the bank," she said. "You'll have your account." In the weeks that followed, the 100% Banking Banner hung prominently in our classroom. My teacher was happy, and the lectures stopped, and the mornings were less fearful for me.

In my eighth grade classroom, I raised my hand one day to ask my teacher to help me with an arithmetic problem which I did not understand.

"Put on your thinking cap," she said to me, and walked away.

A few moments later, the principal's son raised his hand to ask about the same problem. The teacher stopped, sat down, and explained it to him in great detail.

Every few months or so, our teacher would open up her record book to do her paperwork orally.

"John," she would say, "Is your father still working for the city as an engineer?"

John would say, "Yes."

The teacher would make appropriate markings in her book.

Then, she would come to me.

"Is your father still unemployed?"

I would nod. Others would snicker. A girl called me "poor." I never forgot it.

I will never forget my fifth grade teacher and how she made it clear by her actions that she did not like me.

I remember vividly that she used to call upon two children at a time, to work with her in making plaster casts of leaf impressions in clay. It was a fascinating process, and I could hardly wait for my turn. Each day when she chose two children, I knew my chances were coming closer to being a reality. Finally there were but three of us left who had not had a turn.

"Who would like to work with me today?" she asked.

All three of us children raised our hands.

"Tommy and Gail."

Ah well, I thought, I will have a turn tomorrow.

When tomorrow came, she said, "Who has not had a turn?" I raised my hand wildly.

"Well," she said, "then perhaps someone would like another turn."

"All hands went up and my hand was lost.

"But, I haven't had a turn yet!" I sputtered.

"That's why!" she said angrily. "You talked without raising your hand!"

I never did have a turn at that process.

The teacher I will never forget was the one who stood me in the front of the room because I could not remember to invert my fractions. To this day, when I have occasion to invert fractions, I think of that experience and wonder if there was not an alternate way to learning.

I was a new student in a new school. I was shy and terrified by the strangeness of everything that surrounded me.

The teacher announced to the class that she wanted us to write a nonsensical story as our homework assignment.

I thought this was delightful. I had always enjoyed writing and had a measure of success with it at my former school. Hence, the homework assignment went very quickly that evening. But, as the story developed, I found that I could create a nonsensical poem of it. So, I did.

I knew that the poem was a good one, and I was quite pleased with myself when I handed the assignment to the teacher the next morning.

Several days later, when our papers were returned, I noted that all of the other students' papers bore red correction markings, but mine did not.

"We are going to read our stories," the teacher said. "I think we will call upon our new girl to read her story first."

All eyes turned toward me, and I stood fearfully on my feet to begin. The laughter of my classmates was most encouraging, and I found my strength quickly and finished it amid applause.

"Did you write that poem?" the teacher asked me.

"Yes," I said, "I did."

"Think carefully," the teacher said, "*Did* you really write it?"

What was the teacher saying?

"I wrote it," I said.

"No," she countered, "you did not write that poem. You probably read it somewhere and remembered it."

Thereafter, I strived toward more acceptable mediocrity.

28 These Teachers I Will Always Remember

"Gratitude is the heart's memory"—French Proverb.

I had been making an unspectacular academic record until I met my eighth grade teacher. He took me aside one day and told me that I had the potential for making acceptable college entrance grades, if I tried hard enough. Up to that point college appeared as only a dream afforded to the well-heeled and the intellectually gifted, certainly not for a boy of my limited means and "averageness."

He told me that State Colleges were designed for boys like me. "They're not expensive," he said. "I went to a State College myself."

Thereafter, he brought me college catalogs and talked to me about setting up a professional goal. "Think big," he told me. "Anything is possible when you apply yourself."

Because of him, I started taking school seriously. In time I had the necessary grades to enter a State College. Eventually, I graduated with honors, with a degree in engineering.

The years have removed me from my home town, and I have lost contact with my former teacher. However, his counsel remains with me. "Think big," he said. "Anything is possible."

In my present position as a Highway Engineer, I put his words into practical application in the designing of freeways. I could best pay tribute to him by borrowing the epitaph of Christopher Wren in St. Paul's Cathedral: "If you would seek his monument, look around."

The teacher I remember had the reputation for being as ugly as a mud fence. On the first day in her classroom a boy said to me, "Her mouth looks like a torn pocket."

But in a very short time, we students were forgetting that our teacher wasn't the prettiest teacher in the world. The fact was, that we began to think that she was downright handsome!

I remember how she would stand in the front of the classroom with her hand waving slightly in the air like a conductor with a baton in his hands. "Don't give me a 'yes,' and don't give me a 'no.' Tell me *why!*" You had to think in her classroom. You had to have conviction. You had to base conviction on something more than hearsay. Her method of teaching was a new and exciting experience for all of us.

The first time I had ever experienced the beauty of a painted canvas was when she herded all of us tenth graders into a bus and took us to the city art museum. The first time I experienced the beauty of the spoken word was when she played her recordings of Laurence Olivier's interpretation of Hamlet.

She opened doors for me that might possibly have remained closed for the rest of my life—all because she loved people and life and wanted people to share the joy she had found in living.

To this day, when I walk through art museums, I think of her. She is in every Baroque frame—the grand dame of my school experiences, standing head and shoulders above everything else I remember.

I was, and still am, orthopedically handicapped. So, perhaps, it is with just cause that I remember my seventh grade teacher who had one leg shorter than the other. I identified with this teacher who had a physical handicap which was so like my own. It impressed me that a man with a handicap could function so easily in a respected teaching role. I was always secretly proud that other teachers liked him and that the students spoke openly of their admiration toward him. I shared this popularity of his, in a vicarious manner.

With all of this, he was a fine teacher and a whole person. I would judge that I remembered almost everything he said. Chiefly I remembered when he said, "If a man has three legs, it does not necessarily make him a good runner."

I remember my eleventh grade teacher because he gave me the keys to his car so that I could bring him his portfolio.

Up to that time, I did not have a reputation for being particularly trustworthy. That one gesture of trust gave me a sense of well being. It was like feeling suddenly well after a long period of illness. I never forgot how important it is to show someone, sometime in his life, that he is trusted completely.

My ninth grade teacher had the ability to make learning palatable. He was a teacher in the purest sense, but, beyond this, he was humorous. He was able to pace his lectures so that one never had the feeling that the clock had to be watched. More than occasionally, he would interject a funny story. What impressed me most was the fact that his humor was always directed at himself, his shortcomings, and his personal foibles. No one except himself was the object of his humor.

From him I learned that secure people delight in not taking either life or themselves too seriously.

The teacher I will always remember was my home economics instructor.

I was in the eighth grade then and had little leaning toward homemaking as a career.

She told her students, "Homemaking can either be a very dull or a very exciting experience. Let's exploit it for its excitement!"

She made flower arrangements out of common weeds from the fields. She made food so colorful on a table that it looked like a painting from an artist's palette.

I watched the way she would wash off every utensil after using it, never allowing any to pile up on the sink and to create needless work once the meal was finished.

I have been complimented often on my systematic and creative approach to homemaking. She taught me how to find challenge in accepting what she called, "a woman's natural birthright."

The everyday encounters become areas for exploitation. "Make it exciting!" I used to tell myself. Now, it *is* exciting. I thank her often.

I remember my sixth grade teacher who told me that I was a boy who had a natural ability in music. She gave me an old saxophone to take home. "See what you can do with it," she said.

Soon, I was playing it without any formal lessons.

When I left her classroom, I attempted to return the instrument to her.

"Nonsense," she said, "it's yours. It was only collecting dust in my attic."

By the time I was in college, I had a dance band that paid for my room, board, and tuition.

Whenever someone asks me about my formula for success, I tell them about the old sax and the teacher who made it all possible.

The teacher I remember above all others, was my fifth grade teacher who used to surprise us with candy treats whenever a holiday approached. If Easter was coming, we would find yellow candy chicks on our desks. At Halloween, it was pumpkins. I never had a teacher like her before, one who obviously liked kids.

In a personal way, I remember the time she promised to send me a postcard from Europe so that I could add the stamp to my collection. She was as good as her word. In the middle of summer, a postcard arrived from Italy. "Say hello to the other members of the class for me," it said. I took this directive literally and spent the next weeks locating every classmate in order to convey the message, "Our teacher says to say 'hello'!"

Every once in awhile I take out my fifth grade class picture, just to look at it. I never look at it but that I don't find myself laughing out loud. "Look at that smile on my face! Have you ever seen a happier kid?" And why not? I was standing next to my teacher!

29 But You Don't Look Like a Teacher!

A teacher is many things to many people, and many things succinctly stated in colloquy, even to himself:

He is DEDICATED because he realizes that his job will never offer him extensive fame or expanding bank balances, and, in knowing this, he is at once attuned to his role in its highest frequency. He is there to altruistically open doors to potential and to direct that potential, among his students, to betterment of both self and mankind.

He is HUMAN because he realizes that he will make errors in judgment now and again, and these will bring attendant feelings of inadequacy and self-doubt. In knowing this, he will learn to live with his imperfections by, first, identifying them and, then, by attempting to hone them down.

He is PERCEPTIVE because he realizes that quite often the most glaring truths are neither written nor said. In knowing this, he will know *when* to rely upon his feelings, but not necessarily to the consistent exclusion of other measuring devices.

He is RESOURCEFUL because he realizes that if he slips he will take others with him when he falls. In knowing this, he will learn how, in the beginning, to lean heavily on his colleagues and his administrators for the wisdom their experience has given to them, but eventually he will lean wholly on himself and his God-granted endowments of having two feet on which to stand.

He is INDUSTRIOUS because he realizes that only mediocrity and failure require little effort. In knowing this, he will accept the fact that the teaching task *is* work and that a job worth doing, is worth doing well. And anything worth doing well is not accomplished without vast expenditures of time and energies.

He is ORGANIZED because he realizes that haphazardness is commensurate neither with his training nor his intellect, and, in knowing this, he will *plan* in order to make light the task of compressing quality education into one slim teaching day.

He is GOAL-ORIENTED because he realizes that the act of floundering is neither effective nor mature. In knowing this, he will set his goals higher than he dares to expect because he knows the efficacy of stating a desire and in making concrete the stuff of which dreams are made.

He is EMPATHIC because he realizes that he would seek to allieviate child suffering, loneliness, and maladjustment. In knowing this he observes keenly and devises all manner of means to bring relief, happiness, and adjustment where these are most needed, extending this particularly to the new child in his classroom by saying, "I'm certainly glad to see you. We really needed another boy (girl) in this classroom!"

He is CONSISTENT because he realizes that only chaos can develop without the support of follow-through. In knowing this, he is persistent in remembering to reinforce that which he said yesterday so that there will be no doubt in any student's mind, that what he said yesterday will not have a lesser meaning tomorrow.

He is PHILOSOPHICAL because he realizes that perhaps he is not what he should be as a teacher and not what he aspires to be as a teacher. In knowing this, he can look in retrospection as well as in projection and say, "Ah, but I am better than I was yesterday! Tomorrow, I will be better than I am today!"

He is ADULT because he realizes that he is not competing with other instructors in his school, either in terms of popularity or excellence of instruction. In knowing this, he is secure in his own values and ideals, asking not, "Do they like me?" but, rather, "Do I like myself?"

He is RESPONSIBLE because he realizes that careless and irresponsible actions can carry over into his classroom. In knowing this, he is a model for emulation, expecting no more in the way of thoughtful and responsible actions from his students than he, himself, is willing to display inside his classroom and without.

He is HONEST because he realizes that continued application of the word "relativity" can water down morality. In knowing this, he assiduously avoids talking out of both sides of his mouth lest he contribute to the depletion of his own convictions and to the retardation of his own development.

He is KIND because he realizes that, if everyone remembered to do likewise, the ills of society could be erased in one fell swoop, and, in knowing this, he feels the worth of the Golden Rule—not only as it applies to those who people the adult world, but to his students as well.

He is DECISIVE because he realizes that the continual sidestepping of an issue is demoralizing and appears immature to others. In knowing this, he will continue to accumulate his experiences and feed an inquiring mind in order that he may back up his forthright responses.

He is CALM because he realizes that excessive emotional involvement often clouds the issue and brings about the wrong kinds of responses. In knowing this, he will bide his time and count to ten when necessary, in order to give to himself and others the balm of hours and/or days in which either to forget and begin anew or to seek out solutions in a more objective milieu.

He is FLEXIBLE because he realizes that an unyielding position blocks far too many doors both for himself and for others. In knowing this, he occasionally makes the effort to leave the safe harbor of the known if only to test hypotheses and the vastness of his own untapped potential.

He is POSITIVE because he realizes that negativism can destroy the roots of hope and aspiration, not only in himself but in others as well, and in knowing this he will be frugal both in his condemnation and in his use of the word, "no."

He is DIPLOMATIC because he realizes that the truth as he sees it may not necessarily be the truth as others see it. In knowing this he will give himself as well as others a broad margin for arriving at candid appraisals, learning in the interim the value of arbitration and compromise (for the nonce)—not at the expense of his own convictions, but at the expense of his own ego, which occasionally must be termed expendable.

He is ENTHUSIASTIC because he realizes that animated responses from him can be transmitted to his students in a manner somewhat akin to osmosis. In knowing this, he will know with a certainty that the more he gives, the more he, in turn, will receive—the attitude of positive proliferation.

He is ENCOURAGING because he realizes that the fire of a child's ego will often go out when it is left unattended and in knowing this he will stoke the fire and fan the flame, praising and complimenting, often and well.

He is SUPPORTIVE because he realizes that constructive initiative will come back to him a thousandfold. In knowing this he will make the effort, through his words and actions, to change negative impressions—extending this to students, parents, colleagues, administrators, schools, and his profession.

He is MOBILE because he realizes that he must stay in the stream of life both as this applies to his classroom and his way of thinking. In knowing this he will move about in his classroom and his world, even when he feels the inclination to sit; he will sit only when he feels the inclination to lie down.

He is REASONABLE because he realizes that unreasonable demands often bring about unreasonable actions. In knowing this he will apply reasonableness even to his homework assignments, knowing that if he asks for too much involvement, he will end up correcting the parents' work.

He is HUMOROUS because he realizes that he must never take himself or the events of the teaching day too seriously. In knowing this, even the most horrendous of experiences can be reduced to hopeful projection, in saying with conviction, "This too, shall pass."

He is UNBIASED because he realizes that if he slants ideas or prefers individuals he will destroy both creative thinking and trust. In knowing this he will respect all positive, as well as some of the negative, aspects of individualism.

He is ALTRUISTIC because he realizes that much of the good work and success he achieves in the classroom will go unheralded and unseen. In knowing this, he will go right on working toward his long-range and projected goals, just as though he had a bushel basket of accolades.

He is HONORABLE because he realizes that he must never betray the trust that children and parents place in him. In knowing this he will accept the fact that certain areas of home convictions do not bear his tampering, just as certain areas of living experiences within these homes do not bear his investigation or his exploitation: he builds self-concepts; he does not destroy them.

He is SELF-EFFACING because he realizes that, in the long run, he had nothing to do with the distribution of his genes and chromosomes. In knowing this he will continue to put forth his best effort and quietly accept the bouquets as they come, without the tediousness and poor taste of blowing his own horn.

He is DEMOCRATIC because he realizes that he is building a readiness and a respect for citizenship in our free American society. In knowing this he will provide opportunities for positive understandings by involving his students in the democratic processes such as voting and decision making—and, above all, the attendant *responsibilities* of living and working in a free democratic society.

He is DEPENDABLE because he realizes that built into his professional role is a moral responsibility, the acceptance or rejection of which can affect hundreds of lives. In knowing this, he will *do* what he is *supposed to do* when he is supposed to do it, and he will *be* where he is *supposed to be* when he is supposed to be there.

He is COURTEOUS because he realizes that imitation is one of the strongest of learning theories and, in knowing this, he will perpetuate the practice and art of consideration toward others, saying not, "Do as I say!" but, rather, "Do as I am!"

He is a RECORD KEEPER because he realizes that dated and comprehensive data can help to make a judgment less subjective and emotional, and, in knowing this, he is adequately prepared with supporting evidence at times of report cards and parent conferences.

He is SYSTEMATIC because he realizes that a stitch in time will indeed save nine (and perhaps many more). In knowing this, he respects the concept of P&O and establishes routines for such things as correcting papers, setting up displays, and formulating plans for the future.

He is PUNCTUAL because he realizes that school societies strive to operate effectively under the limitations of diversification in time patterns. In knowing this he understands the need for being prompt at scheduled meetings and conferences, as well as for being at his post during supervision assignments in hallways, yards, and in the cafeteria.

He is PROFESSIONAL because he realizes that he has a full and meaningful acceptance of the word involvement, and in knowing this he contributes and supports both his ideas and his presence to professional organizations such as Parent-Faculty Groups and Teachers' Associations.

He is ABOVEBOARD because he realizes that he wishes honor and honorableness, and in knowing this he is ethical in his relations with colleagues and parents, assiduously avoiding such things as gossip, cliques, and lack of support toward the administration.

He is a STUDENT because he realizes that he must never willingly or unwillingly bring about his own personal or professional retrogression and retardation. In knowing this, he is enrolled often in colleges and universities and is also involved in areas of growth and contribution which do not necessarily pertain to his teaching role per se.

He is WHOLE because he realizes that he should seek his strength and his guidance from sources other than those contained in textbooks. In knowing this he has an appreciation for and a commitment toward moral and spiritual values, both as these pertain to himself and as these pertain to others.

He is HIMSELF because he realizes that he will never be like any other teacher he has ever known, before or since, and in knowing this he will learn to assess, evaluate, and appreciate his own uniqueness in his role, both in terms of what he *is* and what he aspires *toward being* in making a personal contribution toward a better world.

Alas, finally, he is *tired*.

He is *poor*.

He is *debt ridden*.

Eventually, *he is old*.

He is retired.

Prithee, *which* president did he teach?

Which *story* was written about him?

Which *movie* was made in cinemascope about his career?

NONE, you say!

Does not *anyone* remember him?

Anyone?

Only *one person* whom he taught?

And, what does *he* say?

He says, "He passed my way,

and I am a better person

for having known him."

He says *that*?

WELL DONE!

WELL DONE!

WELL DONE!

30 Nota Bene!

> I have learned silence from the talkative, toleration from the intolerant, and kindness from the unkind: yet strange, I am ungrateful to these teachers.
>
> —Kahlil Gibran
> *Sand and Foam*